THIS BOOK BELONGS TO B

Holly Chio

FOL 3-

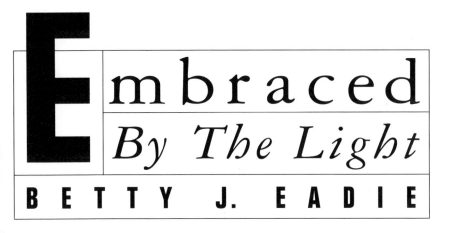

Embraced By The Light

BETTY J. EADIE

With
CURTIS TAYLOR

My appreciation to Curtis Taylor, writer-editor for Gold Leaf Press.

Without his extraordinary talent and tremendous sensitivity to
the Spirit, this book would not exist in its present form.

Betty J. Eadie

GOLD LEAF PRESS

Embraced By The Light

Library of Congress Cataloging-in-Publication Data

    Eadie, Betty Jean (Betty Jean), 1942-
           Embraced by the light / Betty J. Eadie with Curtis Taylor.
              p.   cm.
        ISBN 1-882723-00-7
         1. Near-death experiences.   I. Taylor, Curtis, 1956-
    II. Title.
    BF1045.N4E23   1992
    133.9'01'3—dc20   92-43277
                                                    CIP

Printed in the United States of America

15   14   13   12   11   10

Cover photography and graphics: Mikel Covey

If unavailable in local bookstores, additional copies of this and other
publications by Betty J. Eadie may be purchased by writing the publisher at
the above address.

This book is dedicated:

To The Light, my Lord and Savior Jesus Christ, to whom I owe all that I have. He is the "staff" that I lean on; without him I would fall.

To my wonderful husband Joe, who has been a mortal "rock" of strength and encouragement.

To my eight children: Donna Marie, Cheryl Ann, Glenn Allen, Cynthia Carol, Joseph Lee, Stewart Jeffery, Thomas Britton and Betty Jean, all of whom are the "salt," the flavor, in my life.

And last but not least, to my eight grandchildren: Kurt Andrew, Jessica Elizabeth, Zachary Britton, Natalie Kathleen, Stephanie Leigh, Andrea Meggan, Jennifer Leanne, and Keona Marie.
These little ones are the jewels in my crown.

Acknowledgments

My greatest appreciation and love to my husband. Without his belief in me and his love, this book would have been next to impossible to write. He performed most of the computer duties while patiently giving me a crash course. Then, putting his ego aside, he edited my manuscript. He ate TV dinners and wore his white shirts an extra day so that my time would be free to spend at the keyboard. I love you, Honey. Thank you!

My love and appreciation to my dear friend Nancy Carlisle, whose heart is filled to overflowing with love not only for our Savior, but for all whom she meets. Nancy taught me how to express my love more freely. She showed me her devotion to helping others by spending countless hours with me traveling to speaking engagements, listening over and over to the account of my experience, never tiring of it, and always encouraging me to do more. Nancy was the first to help me lay the foundation for this book, in 1987. Her faith in me never faltered when I gave up those earlier attempts so that I could care for my ill father before his death in July, 1991.

I am indeed indebted to Jane Barfuss, who, after attending three of my talks wrote an account of my near-death experience titled "Spirit World." Those notes have literally traveled around the world. As a direct result of Jane's notes I have met many wonderful people who encouraged me to finish this book—and to write in greater detail.

Contents

Foreword

I learned more about near-death experiences from reading *Embraced By The Light* than from any other experience in my life, including ten years of studying near-death experiences and interviewing children and adults who have survived clinical death. *Embraced By The Light* is not just Betty Eadie's story of dying during surgery and coming back to life; it is actually a journey into the meaning of this life. I remember a young boy who said to his parents after surviving cardiac arrest: "I have a wonderful secret to tell you—I have been climbing a staircase to heaven." That young man was too young to explain what he meant. This book contains that same wonderful secret. It is not a secret about life after death; it is a secret about life.

A near-death experience is in fact the dying experience. We will all have one when we die—rich or poor, murderer or saint. I used to think that when we die, we simply enter into darkness and end our lives. As a critical care physician I had seen many children and adults die and never had any reason to think otherwise. It was only after I took the time to ask those who survived clinical death what the experience was like did I learn that the process of dying is often joyous and spiritual. Darkness does not await us at the end of life, but rather a loving light—a light, one child said, that "has a lot of good things in it."

Near-death experiences are not caused by a lack of oxygen to the brain, or drugs, or psychological stresses evoked by the fear of dying. Almost twenty years of scientific research has documented that these experiences are a natural and normal process. We have even documented an area in the brain which allows us to have the experience. That means that near-death experiences are absolutely real and not hallucinations of the mind. They are as real as any other human capability; they are as real as math, as real as language.

It has only been eight years since my research group at the University of Washington and Seattle Children's Hospital published this information in the American Medical Association's Pediatric journals. Although this research has been replicated by researchers throughout the world, including by the University of Florida, Boston Children's Hospital, and by the University of Ultrech in the Netherlands, it is not yet widely understood by the general population. Unfortunately, our society has not yet accepted the scientific advances in understanding the dying process which have occurred in the past two decades. We desperately need to reeducate ourselves that we are spiritual beings as well as biological machines. So many of our society's problems, including the crisis in health care, death with dignity, the cult of greed which has bankrupted our economy, the national shame of homeless women and children, all stem from a lack of understanding that we are spiritual beings who are mutually dependent upon each other.

Embraced By The Light teaches us that our own individual lives are important and filled with meaning. I am struck again and again that those who have entered into God's light at the end of life return with a simple and beautiful message: "Love is supreme. . . . Love must govern. . . . We create our own surroundings by the thoughts we think. . . . We are sent here to live life fully, to live it abundantly, to find joy in our own creations, to experience both failure and success, to use free will to expand and magnify our lives." Betty does not return from clinical death with grandiose claims of establishing a new church or of producing miracle cures for diseases, but rather with a simple message of love. The meaning of the near-death experience is one that we all know is true, but one that we have forgotten: "We are to love one another. We are to be kind, to be tolerant, to give generous service."

This book is really a textbook of the near-death experience, written as a simple and wonderful story that we can all understand. I have never had a near-death experience, or even a spiritual experience that I can identify, and I was somewhat skeptical of what many people were sharing with me. Certainly the hardest part for the skeptic who wants to understand is comprehending what it is like to be out of the physical body or how death can be a pleasant experience. Betty Eadie's book illustrates the stages of the experience with superb writing that bridges this gap; she makes the unknowable comprehensible.

As she started to die, she felt her body become weaker and weaker. Then "I felt a surge of energy, a pop or release inside me. My first impression was that I was free. There was nothing unnatural about the experience." She then met guardian spirits who helped her to understand important things about her life and then to comprehend her relationship with her family. They assisted her in her transition into death. She entered into darkness and traveled in a dark tunnel. "I thought this must be where the valley of the shadow of death is," she says. "I had never felt greater tranquility in my life."

Her experience answers questions that people have had for me for years about near-death experiences—questions I have never been able to answer. She describes her life review on the other side and how she was not judged by others, but rather by herself. She explains the meaning and causes of some negative near-death experiences and why some people are deeply troubled by their experience. She explains why life is often difficult and why bad things often happen to good people. She explains why people who have died are often reluctant to return to the body. "The body's cumbersome weight and coldness were abhorrent," she says. "After the joy of spiritual freedom, I had become a prisoner of the flesh again."

Betty not only had a near-death experience as an adult, but she was prepared for it by having a near-death experience as a child. Children have simple and pure near-death experiences, untroubled by religious or cultural expectations. They do not suppress the experience as adults often do and have no trouble accepting the spiritual implications of seeing God. I will never forget a five year old girl who shyly told me: "I talked to Jesus and he was nice. He told me that it wasn't my time to die." Children remember their near-death experiences far more often than adults do, and as a result of their experience they seem to have an easier time accepting and understanding their own spirituality as adults. If they have another near-death experience as an adult, it is usually exceptionally powerful and complete.

Betty Eadie reminds us that the importance of near-death experiences is what they teach us about living. It has only been in the past few hundred years that we have decided that there is no spirit in man—and therefore no life after death. This has led directly to an unnatural fear of dying which permeates our lives and prevents us from living life to its fullest. Betty teaches us that the knowledge that dying is spiritual leads not to a desire to die, but rather to a desire to live life more completely. "Now I knew that there actually was a God," she says. "No longer did I believe in just a Universal Power. . . . I saw a loving being who created the universe. . . ."

One little girl told me that when she died, she learned "I had a new life." She told me that although she had heard about heaven in Sunday School, she really didn't believe it. After she died and came back to life, she felt, "I am not afraid to die anymore, because I kind of know a little more about it now." She did not want to die again, but rather, she learned that "life is for living and light is for later." I asked her how she was different because of her experience, and she paused for a long time and said: "It's nice to be nice."

Embraced By The Light teaches us the same lesson: "If we are kind, we will have joy." Betty asked Jesus, "Why didn't I know this before?" And she was told, "Before you can feel joy, you must know sorrow." This simple statement has changed the way I understand life. It is something that I did know "before"; in fact, I had heard it all my life. I realize, after reading Betty's book, that my own life has been changed by it, that I need to reconnect with simple truths that I have always known but have ignored.

As a Native American Indian, Betty attended a boarding school as a child. In front of the school was a large sign which said: "Where there is no vision, the people perish." Our society has lost understanding of its own spiritual beliefs and visions. This has directly led to the ghoulish mess we have made of dying, where patients die hidden away in hospitals in the cold company of machines, not in the company of relatives and friends. We have forgotten how to die, as it is no longer a part of our ordinary lives. At the same time, we have forgotten how to live. Joseph Campbell, the great mythologist, stated that many of our modern problems, from drug addiction to the violence in our inner cities come directly from our collective lack of spiritual vision. We have forgotten that our ordinary lives are spiritually important.

There is a great secret contained in *Embraced By The Light*. It is a secret that you already know. It is something that the great prophets and spiritual leaders have tried to tell us for thousands of years. Betty Eadie learned it by nearly dying. It has the power to change your life.

MELVIN MORSE, M.D.

The First Night

Something was wrong. My husband, Joe, had left my hospital room only a few minutes before, but already a foreboding feeling was enveloping me. I would be alone through the night, alone on the eve of one of my most frightening challenges. Thoughts of death began creeping into my mind. Thoughts like these had not come to me in years. Why were they so pervasive now?

It was the evening of November 18, 1973. I had entered the hospital to undergo a partial hysterectomy. As a thirty-one year-old mother of seven who was in otherwise excellent health, I had chosen to follow my doctor's advice to have the operation. Both my husband, Joe, and I felt comfortable with the decision.

I still felt comfortable with the decision, but something else was bothering me now—something unidentifiable.

In our years of marriage we had rarely spent nights apart, and I tried to reflect on our family and the special closeness we enjoyed. Although we had six children at home (one had died of Sudden Infant Death Syndrome when she was an infant) we were sometimes reluctant to leave them. Even on our "date nights" we would stay home and let the children plan our dates for us. Sometimes they catered a dinner for us, providing candlelight in the living room with a fire crackling in the fireplace. We usually had just the right music too—maybe not the music we would have chosen but perfect nonetheless. I recalled the evening they served us Chinese food on a decorated coffee table and provided large pillows for us to sit on. They turned the lights down low, kissed us goodnight, and giggled as they hurried up the stairs. Joe and I seemed to have found a little bit of heaven on earth.

I reflected on how lucky I was to have a companion as loving and considerate as Joe. He had taken vacation from work to be with me before I went into the hospital, and he planned to spend another week at home while I recuperated. He and our two oldest daughters, who were fifteen and fourteen, were already making plans for a wonderful Thanksgiving dinner.

The feelings of foreboding settled more heavily upon me. Perhaps it was the darkness of the room, the terrible darkness I had learned to dread as a girl. Or maybe these ominous feelings came from another experience, an experience in a hospital years ago which still filled me with questions–and wonder.

When I was four years old, my parents had just separated. My father used to say that "marrying an Indian woman back in those days was probably the worse thing a white man could do." He was a fair-haired Scotch-Irishman, and she was a full-blooded Sioux Indian. As the seventh of ten children, I hardly had a chance to know either parent before they separated. My mother went back to live on the reservation, and my father went to live with his parents in town. At that time, six of us children were placed in a Catholic boarding school.

It was while at the boarding school that first winter that I developed a terrible cough and began shivering constantly. Forty girls shared one large room, and I remember leaving my bed one night and getting into my sister Joyce's bed. We lay together and cried—I in my fever and she in fear for me. When one of the Sisters came by on her nightly rounds, she discovered me and took me back to my bed, which was damp and cold with perspiration. Joyce tried to convince the Sister of my illness but was unsuccessful. Finally on the third night I was taken to a hospital.

The doctor diagnosed me with whooping cough and double pneumonia, and he told a nurse to contact my parents. I remember him telling her that he didn't expect me to live through the night. As I lay on the bed, burning with fever, I seemed to slip in and out of sleep. Once, I felt hands on my head, and looking up, I saw a nurse leaning over me. She ran her hands through my hair and said, "She's just a baby." I'll never forget the kindness I felt in these words. I snuggled further down into the covers and felt warm and content. Her words gave me peace, and I closed my eyes to sleep again.

I awoke to the doctor's words: "It's too late. We've lost her," and I felt the covers pulled up over my head. I was confused. Why was it too late? I turned my head and looked around the room, which didn't seem to be an odd thing, even though the covers were pulled over my face. I saw the doctor and nurse standing by the bed. I looked around the room and noticed that it was filled with brighter light than before. The bed seemed huge to me, and I remember thinking, "I'm like a little brown bug in this big white bed." Then the doctor walked away and I became aware of another presence nearby. Suddenly I wasn't lying on the bed but found myself in someone's arms. I looked up and saw a man with a beautiful white beard looking at me. His beard fascinated me. It seemed to sparkle with a bright light, a light that came from within the beard. I giggled and ran my hands through the beard and twirled it on my fingers. I felt perfectly calm and happy with him. He gently rocked me, cradling me in his arms, and although I didn't know who he was, I never wanted to leave him.

"She's breathing again!" the nurse called out and the doctor came running back into the room. But it was a different room. I had been moved into a smaller one that was very dark. The man with the white beard was gone. My body was wet with fever, and I was scared. The doctor turned the light on, and they took me back into the first room.

When my parents arrived, they were told that they had almost lost me. I heard the words but still didn't understand them. How could I have been lost if I was there the whole time? But it was good to be with my parents again, with people who really knew me and loved me—like the man with the white beard. I asked them who that man was and where he had gone, but they didn't understand what I was talking about. I told them about the doctor saying that it was too late and how the man with the white light in his beard had come and held me, but they had no answers. They never did. This experience would be mine to cherish as an oasis of love throughout my young life. The memory has never changed, and each time I remember it I get a sense of the calmness and happiness I had in his arms.

I tried to recall these memories now as darkness seeped into my room. Since those early days away from my parents, darkness had terrified me. Now, alone in the darkness again, a strange feeling was in the room. Death seemed to swirl everywhere around me. My thoughts became filled with it, caught up in it. Death. Death and God. These two seemed eternally linked. What awaited me on the other side? If I were to die tomorrow, what would I find? Eternal death? Eternity with a vengeful God? I wasn't sure. And what was God like? I only hoped that he was *not* what I had learned as a child in boarding school.

I can still remember details of that first school building with its gigantic brick walls and dark, cold rooms. A chain-link fence separated the boys' dormitory from the girls', and another fence ran along the perimeter of the school. We were locked in from the world, and away from each other. I still remember that first morning when my brothers were ushered to one building while my sisters and I were led to another. I'll never forget the fear in their eyes as they looked back at us one last time. I thought my heart would break.

My two sisters and I were taken to a small room where the nuns de-loused us in chemicals and cut our hair. Then they gave us two dresses each, one color for one week, the other for the following week. These uniforms would help identify runaways. Our oldest sister, Thelma, whom we called Sis, was separated from us and sent to another room for older girls. That first night Joyce and I lined up with the other girls and marched into the room where we stood by our beds until the Sister blew a whistle. Then we got promptly into bed, the light was clicked off, and the door was locked from the outside. Being locked inside this big darkened room horrified me. In the dark I waited in terror until sleep finally, gratefully, overcame me.

On Sunday all of the children attended church, which offered my sisters and me the possibility of seeing our brothers on the other side of the chapel. As I fought through the crush of girls to get a glimpse of my brothers that first Sunday, I felt a knock on my head. I turned around and saw a long pole with a rubber ball on the end. The Sisters used this instrument to correct our behavior in church, and this would be only the first of many times I felt it. Because I found it difficult to understand what the bells meant and when I should kneel, I was tapped by the pole often. Still, though, I *was* able to see my brothers, and this was worth any punishment from the ball.

We were taught about God there, and I learned many things I had never considered. We were told that we—the Indians—were heathens and sinners, and, of course, I believed this. The nuns were supposed to be special in God's eyes, and we learned that they were there to help us. My sister Thelma was often beaten by them with a little hose and was then forced to thank the Sister who had done it or be beaten again. These were God's chosen servants, as I believed, and I began to fear God immensely because of them. Everything I learned about him intensified this fear. He seemed angry and impatient and very powerful, which meant that he would probably destroy me or send me straight to hell on Judgment Day—or before then if I crossed him. This boarding-school god was a being I hoped never to meet.

I looked at the large clock on the wall. Only minutes had gone by since Joe had left. *Only minutes.* The tiny light above the sink in my room produced only enough light to create dark shadows—shadows which hung in my imagination like nightmares from my past. My mind must be racing, I thought. Propelled by my isolation, my mind was racing through the dark corridors of my memories. I had to control it in order to find peace or the night would be endless. I settled myself and tried to find happier thoughts from my past.

A ray of light began to shine.

*   *   *

Brainerd Indian Training School was run by Wesleyan Methodists. I'll never forget reading on my first day there the large sign that stood in front of the school: "Where there is no vision the people perish." I thought, of course, that the sign referred to the Indians and that since this was a training school, we were there to be trained to have more vision. This idea was probably reinforced by other signs I saw in town, such as: "No Indians or Dogs Allowed."

Brainerd Indian Training School proved to be a more positive experience than my earlier ones had been. We enjoyed a cozy, less formal atmosphere, and the teachers seemed to appreciate being around the students. I learned that God meant different things to different people. Instead of the angry, vengeful God that I had come to know before, these people taught of a happier God who was pleased when we were happy. In our devotionals people often shouted Amen and hallelujah, and it took a while to get used to their sudden outbursts. Although I recognized that there were different ways to view God and to worship him, I think I remained convinced that he was still the God who would punish me if I ever died and appeared before him.

During summers I attended both Lutheran and Baptist churches and occasionally the Salvation Army. Where I attended church then did not seem as important as the fact that I went. My curiosity about God grew as I matured because I recognized that he was playing a major role in my life. I just wasn't sure what that role was or how it would affect me as I grew older. I approached him in prayer to get answers, but I didn't feel that he heard me. My words just seemed to dissipate in the air. When I was eleven I summoned my courage and asked our school matron if she really believed that there was a god. I felt that if anybody really *knew*, she did. But instead of answering my question, she slapped me and asked how dare I question his existence. She told me to get to my knees and pray for forgiveness, which I did. But now I knew that I was doomed to hell because of my lack of faith—because I had questioned the existence of God. I was sure now that I could never be forgiven.

Later that summer I moved back in with my father and had an experience that paralyzed me with fear. One night after getting in bed I opened the curtains to the window next to me and lay there gazing at the stars and passing clouds, something I had enjoyed doing since very young. Suddenly my eye caught a ray of white light coming down from a cloud, and I was frozen with fear. It moved from side to side as if it were searching for us, for anybody. I knew that this was Jesus coming in his Second Coming, and I screamed at the top of my lungs. I had been taught that he would come as a thief in the night and would take the righteous with him and burn the wicked. It was hours before my father could calm me, finally convincing me that I had only seen a search light advertising the arrival of a carnival in town. It was the first search light I had ever seen. I closed the curtain and didn't star gaze for some time.

My search for the true nature of God continued. I remember attending various churches and memorizing many scriptures from the New Testament. I came to believe that when a person died, his spirit would remain in the grave with the body until resurrection day, when Christ would come and the righteous would rise up to be with him. I thought of this often, still dreading my own death and the blackness that would follow.

The Night Deepens

The curtains of my hospital room were closed now. Had I closed them? I looked at the clock again, then almost got up to see if it was unplugged. Time seemed to stand still. I needed to talk to someone. Perhaps a nurse would come visit with me, or better yet, I could call home. I reached across the bed and got the phone. Moments later it was ringing, and Donna, our fifteen-year-old, answered it. She immediately asked if I was okay. It was wonderful to hear the concern in her voice. I told her that everything was fine but that I was a little lonely. "Dad isn't home yet," she said. My heart dropped. I wanted so desperately to talk to him. "Mom? Are you okay?," she asked, and I said, "Yes, I'm fine." But what I wanted to say was "Please, get Dad and send him back! Get him here as soon as you can!" My apprehensions were growing.

I heard little voices over the phone: "I want to talk to Mom." "Hey, give me the phone!" "I'll tell Dad!" And the sounds of home made me feel better. I spent the next half hour saying goodnight to each child. But when I hung up the loneliness fell on me again like a blanket. The room seemed darker, and the distance between the hospital and our home felt more like a million miles than just across town. My family was life itself to me, and being away from them scared me, hurt me. But as I thought again of each of my children, and of course of my husband, Joe, I felt better, and at that point nobody in the world could have convinced me that in only hours I wouldn't care if I ever returned home to them again—that in fact, I would be begging *not* to return to them.

I had always thought that my husband and children would eventually replace the family I had missed in my childhood. I had promised myself that when I married and began my own family that they would be my prime interest and my greatest refuge.

I promised myself that I would love my husband and remain with him through thick and thin, and that our children would always be able to count on us being together.

When I turned fifteen I was sent to live with my mother. My father felt that a maturing young lady should be with her mother—not in a boarding school or with him. My mother found also that she needed a babysitter while she worked full time. So, I was taken out of school and stayed at home to care for my youngest sister. As I spent each day at home I began to feel sorry for myself, watching the neighborhood kids go to school in the mornings and come home in the afternoons. I wasn't fully aware yet of what an education would mean to me as I got older, but I knew that I missed the companionship of friends and my other brothers and sisters. Within a short time I began to feel that the only way out was for me to get married and start a family of my own. I felt that my life was controlled by the needs of others and that I was losing the right to any personal happiness. I wanted clothes of my own, a bed of my own, a home of my own. I wanted a husband I could trust, one who would always love me no matter what happened in our lives.

It was no wonder then that I fell hopelessly in love with the boy next door and married him the following spring. My father was adamantly against it, but I was living with my mother, and she supported it. I was fifteen and very naive as to what the demands of a real family were. The immaturity of us both, and the fact that we had vastly different goals in life, ended our marriage six years later. My dream was broken, and I had a wounded soul that would take a lot of patience and love to heal. I have never regretted this marriage, though, because it gave me four beautiful children. My first were two girls, Donna and Cheryl, and then I had a son, Glenn. Our youngest, Cynthia, died at three months of SIDS.

I met Joe at a dance the Christmas following my divorce. He was stationed at Stead Air Force Base near Reno, Nevada, where I was then living. Joe too had been through a divorce, and as I got to know him I found that we had a lot in common. He had a background similar to my own and also a desire for a strong family unit. We seemed to fit somehow. Even my children wanted him to be with us, perhaps more than I did at first, and the time came rapidly when we married.

From the beginning it seemed almost too good to be true. Joe had a tenderness about him that I had not experienced before. He was tremendously patient with the children, yet firm enough that they responded to his love. They fought over who would be first at the door to greet him when he returned from work at night. Joe was "Dad" to them from the beginning—in every way.

We *wanted* to remain together, and that, combined with our growing maturity, is the glue that has held us together through the years. As we moved from place to place, and as we adjusted in our own lives, we simply made the commitment to work things out and keep our family together, no matter what the cost. Our desires were to the family first and ourselves second.

In July of 1963, Joe was transferred to Randolph Air Force Base, in San Antonio, Texas. Computers were making their debut, and Joe was reassigned to learn computer programming. During our four years in Texas I gave birth to two boys, Joseph Jr., and Stewart Jeffery.

We were living a dream come true. We had a new car and a new house *complete with air conditioning.* The kids had plenty of clothes, and I was able to stay home and care for them. I truly felt blessed. The security and joy I felt now seemed an eternity away from the boarding schools and loneliness of my childhood and broken marriage. But still, I knew that something was missing.

I still prayed, but my relationship with God seemed distant and filled with fear. I knew that he had answered my prayers from time to time—such as after my divorce; when I had prayed for someone loving and patient to help me raise my children, he had literally led me to Joe. I believed that God was real and loved his children—despite his professed vengeance—but I had no idea how to incorporate that love into my life or how to share it with my children. I discussed the matter with Joe and suggested that we begin attending a church. He was less than enthusiastic, mostly because of earlier experiences that had disillusioned him about religion. I respected his position but still sought a way to bring a stronger sense of religious belief into our family. We attended a few local churches, but we didn't feel satisfied, and after a while I just let things go. My beliefs about religion would remain uncertain for many years.

The nurse came into my room and interrupted my thoughts. She had a little cup of sleeping pills, but I refused them because of my aversion to almost any type of medication. My fear of drugs went back a long way, and I seldom even took aspirin, preferring instead to tough out a headache or illness. The nurse went out of the room, and I was left again with my thoughts. In the utter loneliness of the night, my thoughts now turned to the surgery just hours away. Would everything be all right? I had heard many stories of people dying on the operating table. Would I be another? Images of graveyards filled my mind. I conjured up scenes of tombstones and crosses around skeletons' necks in buried coffins. I began wondering about the last rites, something I had heard about in my youth. I tried to figure out why the dead wore crosses. Was it to show God that they were saints? Or were they sinners who needed protection from the demons of hell? Gloom settled more strongly upon me, the darkness still tugging at me, and I reached over to the buzzer and called the nurse.

"Do you have any of those pills handy?" I asked when she came in. She gave me a puzzled look for a moment, but she got the pills for me. I took them and thanked her as she turned down the lights and shut the door. It was a while before I felt drowsy, and, finally, I said my prayers and went to sleep.

The Second Day

*M*orning came quickly, with the sunlight sneaking around the edges of the curtains. The surgery was scheduled for noon. I could either wake up and wait for hours, or I could enjoy the luxury of sleeping in. I was still groggy from the sleeping pill, or perhaps I was exhausted from my fear and anxiety of the night before. Now with the morning light brightening the room, I relaxed and began to reflect on the last time I had been in a hospital. My fears of the previous night had been slight compared to my fears then. At least this time I knew what was *supposed* to happen.

*   *   *

The Second Day

Joe retired from the Air Force in 1967, and we had looked at the many options open to him in a new civilian career. Computers were becoming a new industry in themselves, and his training qualified him to begin a new career just about anywhere he wanted. All we had to decide was which side of the country we wanted to live on. We finally chose to move to the Pacific Northwest, where Joe would take a position at a large aerospace corporation. We felt that the climate would be a welcome contrast to the hot, dry weather we had become accustomed to in Texas. Also, we would be able to live near my father and his wife, who now lived in the Northwest.

Shortly after moving there, I became pregnant with our seventh child. This was not the kind of surprise we wanted. Feeling that we had all the children we could properly care for—five children living—we had taken precautions to prevent another pregnancy. My six previous pregnancies had weakened my body, and the doctors had discouraged me from having another child.

In the third month I began experiencing severe cramping and bleeding. The doctors told me that I was passing fetal tissue. Because of this and other complications, they were sure that I would miscarry soon. I was admitted to the hospital for a week as the bleeding continued. We waited for my body to dispose of the damaged fetus naturally. Soon, it became apparent that the pregnancy was not going to terminate, and one of the doctors suggested that I consider aborting it. He believed that the baby, if carried to term, would most likely be born with parts of its body missing. I had no reason to doubt him. After discussing it with Joe, we decided to undergo the surgery.

The day before the scheduled abortion I was in the hospital to be examined by another team of doctors, and they were in agreement that we should continue as planned. Just as the last doctor passed by me to leave the room, he said, "We don't understand why that little fellow is hanging in there." I felt a chill pass through me, and the thought came to me, "Don't do this. You must have this child. He wants to be born."

When Joe came to visit me at the hospital that evening, I explained what the doctors had said and told him about my impressions that this child should be born. We talked about going ahead with the pregnancy and having a deformed child. Neither of us wanted to do it, but I knew that I couldn't live with myself if I aborted this child now. Joe agreed that we had to keep it, and we met later that night with the doctors and explained our feelings. They were adamant. We must abort the damaged fetus. They said that no doctor would approve the continuation of the pregnancy, and that they, certainly, wouldn't be a part of it.

I was discharged from the hospital the next day and began looking for a doctor who would accept me on my terms. I finally found a young doctor who had just begun his private practice after spending several years in the Air Force. He felt a kinship with Joe because of their common background and agreed to take me on as a patient. He saw some possibility that the baby might live but he too was afraid it would be born deformed. He put me to bed and gave me a list of orders to follow.

Joe and the kids were great in filling in for me around the house, and I used the time to take some home study courses and finish my high school education. As the months flew by and we rapidly approached my due date, I became increasingly frightened. We prepared the children for the likely outcome, that the baby would be born either deformed, possibly with parts of its body missing, or it could die. Joe and I tried to comfort each other by recalling often my impressions upon hearing the doctor's words: "This little fellow is still hanging in there." This was during the times when hospitals didn't allow fathers in delivery rooms, and the thought of facing this child's birth without Joe near me was terrifying. Though the hospital staff agreed to let Joe stay with me during the delivery, they were apprehensive about Joe's possible reaction to it. They told him that if he fainted or became ill during the experience that their first responsibility would be to me. He was asked to sign a waiver that exempted them from liability for him.

Labor began and I entered the hospital on June 19, 1968. I was so frightened that my body shook uncontrollably. Joe stood by me in the delivery room holding my hand and stroking my head. He had to wear a green gown and white mask like the doctors. His gray-blue eyes tried to comfort me, but I could tell by the puffing in and out of the mask that he was as terrified as I was. As delivery approached we tightly clutched hands.

As the baby was born, I watched the doctor's eyes. I knew immediately that our months of fear and anguish had been in vain. He laid the baby on my stomach so I could hold it, and Joe and I quickly looked it over from head to toe. We began crying. Our son was as perfect and healthy as any baby ever born. I knew as I held him that, indeed, this baby was meant to come to me, and that it did, very much, want to be born.

Although I would not have changed my decision for anything, the pregnancy took a toll on my body. Over the next few years a multitude of problems developed, and my doctor suggested that I have a hysterectomy. After thoughtfully considering it and discussing it with Joe, I decided to go along with the doctor's recommendation, and the date for my surgery was set.

Now, the morning of the surgery, a new nurse came in and prodded me awake. She wanted to give me a shot to put me back to sleep in preparation for the surgery. I was amused that she was waking me up to put me back to sleep. I probably would have laughed, but I was already feeling the drug working through my veins with its warmth spreading throughout my body. The doctor must have come in about then because I heard his voice say: "Is she ready?" And everything quietly became black.

It was afternoon before I regained some awareness. My doctor was standing by me, saying that the surgery had been a success and that I should be feeling fine shortly. And I remember thinking to myself, "This is great. Now I can finally get some rest and stop worrying about the surgery." And I fell back to sleep.

That night, I awoke and looked around me. Although I was in a semi-private room, I was alone. The other bed was empty. The room was cheerfully decorated, with brightly striped orange and yellow wallpaper. Loud, I thought, but cheerful. I noticed two night stands, two closets, a television set, and a large window near my bed. I had asked for a window because ever since my childhood I had suffered from claustrophobia. It was dark outside, and the only light in the room was the night light over the sink by the door. I rang for the nurse and asked for some water. She said I had been given ice chips since earlier that afternoon, but I had no recollection of getting any. And she said that my husband and some friends had been in and visited with me, but I couldn't recall seeing them. I *was* conscious of the fact, however, that my makeup was a mess and that I really didn't appreciate anybody seeing me when I didn't know about it. And then there was my gown; as I looked down I realized that it covered only the *bare* essentials. I would have to talk to Joe about bringing his friends around.

At nine o'clock the nurse brought my evening medication. Except for a little pain from the surgery, I felt fine. I took the pills and settled down to watch a little television before sleeping. I must have dozed off because when I looked at the clock again it was nine-thirty, and I was suddenly feeling light-headed and had the sudden urge to call Joe. I found the phone and somehow managed to dial him. I do not remember the conversation—I was becoming so tired that all I wanted to do was sleep. I managed to turn off the television set, then pull the blanket up under my neck. I was beginning to feel chilled to my bones and weaker than I had ever felt before.

My Death

Again, I must have dozed for a while, but not for long because the clock still seemed to say nine-thirty. Then suddenly I woke up with the strangest feeling. Somehow, my instincts warned me of impending danger. I looked around the room. The door had been pulled half-closed. The dimmed light was still on over the small sink by the door. I felt myself become keenly alert and growing in fear. My senses told me that I was alone, and I could feel my body becoming weaker and weaker.

I reached for the cord near the bed in an attempt to call the nurse. But try as I might, I could not bring myself to move. I felt a terrible sinking sensation, like the very last drops of blood were being drained from me. I heard a soft buzzing sound in my head and continued to sink until I felt my body become still and lifeless.

Then I felt a surge of energy. It was almost as if I felt a pop or release inside me, and my spirit was suddenly drawn out through my chest and pulled upward, as if by a giant magnet. My first impression was that I was free. There was nothing unnatural about the experience. I was above the bed, hovering near the ceiling. My sense of freedom was limitless and it seemed as if I had done this forever. I turned and saw a body lying on the bed. I was curious about who it was, and immediately I began descending toward it. Having worked as an LPN, I knew well the appearance of a dead body, and as I got closer to the face I knew at once that it was lifeless. And then I recognized that it was my own. That was *my* body on the bed. I wasn't taken aback, and I wasn't frightened; I simply felt a kind of sympathy for it. It appeared younger and prettier than I remembered, and now it was dead. It was as if I had taken off a used garment and had put it aside forever, which was sad because it was still good—there was still a lot of use left in it. I realized that I had never seen myself three-dimensionally before; I had only seen myself in the mirror, which is only a flat surface. But the eyes of the spirit see in more dimensions than the eyes of the mortal body. I saw my body from all directions at once—from in front, behind, and from the sides. I saw aspects to my features I had never known before, adding a wholeness, a completeness to my view. This may be why I didn't recognize myself at first.

My new body was weightless and extremely mobile, and I was fascinated by my new state of being. Although I had felt pain from the surgery only moments before, I now felt no discomfort at all. I was whole in every way—perfect. And I thought, "This is who I really am."

My attention went back to the body. I realized that nobody was aware that I had died, and I felt an urgency to tell somebody. "I'm dead," I thought, "and no one is here to know it!" But before I could move, three men suddenly appeared at my side. They wore beautiful, light brown robes, and one of them had a hood on the back of his head. Each wore a gold-braided belt that was tied about the waist with the ends hanging down. A kind of glow emanated from them, but not unusually bright, and then I realized that a soft glow came from my own body and that our lights had merged together around us. I was not afraid. The men appeared to be about seventy or eighty years old, but I knew somehow that they were on a time scale different than earth's. The impression came to me that they were much older than seventy or eighty years old—that they were ancient. I sensed in them great spirituality, knowledge, and wisdom. I believe they appeared to me in robes to evoke the impression of these virtues. I began to think of them as monks—mostly because of the robes—and I knew that I could trust them. They spoke to me.

They had been with me for "eternities," they said. I didn't fully understand this; I had a difficult time comprehending the concept of eternity, let alone eternities. Eternity to me had always been in the future, but these beings said they had been with me for eternities in the past. This was more difficult to comprehend. Then I began to see images in my mind of a time long ago, of an existence before my life on earth, of my relationship with these men "before." As these scenes unfolded in my mind I knew that we had indeed known each other for "eternities." I became excited. The fact of a pre-earth life crystallized in my mind, and I saw that death was actually a "rebirth" into a greater life of understanding and knowledge that stretched forward and backward through time. And I knew that these were my choicest friends in that greater life and that they had chosen to be with me. They explained that they, with others, had been my guardian angels during my life on earth. But I felt these three were special, that they were also my "ministering angels."

They said that I had died prematurely. They somehow communicated a feeling of peace and told me not to worry, that everything would be all right. As this feeling came to me, I sensed their deep love and concern. These feelings and other thoughts were communicated from spirit to spirit—from intelligence to intelligence. At first, I thought that they were using their mouths, but this was because I was used to people "speaking." They communicated much more rapidly and completely, in a manner they referred to as "pure knowledge." The closest word in English we would have to define it is telepathy, but even that doesn't describe the full process. I felt their emotions and intents. I *felt* their love. I experienced their feelings. And this filled me with joy because they loved me so much. My earlier language, the language of my body, was truly limited, and I realized that my former ability to express feelings had been almost nonexistent compared with the ability of the spirit to communicate in this pure way.

There were many things that they wanted to share with me, and that I wanted to share with them, but we all knew that the concerns of the moment took precedence. I suddenly thought of my husband and children and was worried as to how my death would affect them. How could my husband care for six children? How would the children get along without me? I needed to see them again, at least to satisfy my own concerns.

My only thought was to leave the hospital and go to my family. After so many years of waiting for a family, of working to keep my family together, I was afraid that now I would lose them. Or, perhaps, I was afraid that they would lose me.

Immediately I began to look for an exit, and I spotted the window. I quickly went through it and emerged outside. Soon, I would learn that I didn't need to use the window, that I could have left the room at any point. It was only because of my linger-ing thoughts (and therefore limitations) of mortality that I thought of using the window. It occurred to me that I was in a "slow moving mode" because I still thought in terms of having my physical body, when in fact my spiritual body could move through anything that had been solid to me before. The window had been closed the whole time.

My trip home was a blur. I began moving at tremendous speed, now that I realized I could, and I was only vaguely aware of trees rushing below me. I made no decisions, gave myself no directions—just thought of home and knew I was going there. Within a moment I was at my house and found myself entering the living room.

I saw my husband sitting in his favorite armchair reading the newspaper. I saw my children running up and down the stairs and knew that they were supposed to be getting ready for bed. Two of them were in a pillow fight—actually normal bedtime procedure for our children. I had no desire to communicate with them, but I was concerned about their lives without me. As I watched them individually, a preview of sorts ran through my mind about them, enabling me to see ahead into each of their lives. I came to know that each of my children was on earth for their own experiences, that although I had thought of them as "mine," I had been mistaken. They were individual spirits, like myself, with an intelligence that was developed before their lives on earth. Each one had their own free will to live their life as they chose. I knew that this free will should not be denied them. They had only been placed in my care. Although I don't recall them now, I knew that my children had their own life agendas and that when they had completed them, they too would end their stay on earth. I foresaw some of their challenges and difficulties but knew that these would be necessary for their growth. There was no need for sorrow or fear. In the end each of my children would be all right, and I knew that it would be only a brief moment before we were all together again. I felt bathed in serenity. My husband and my precious children, this family I had waited so long for, would be all right. I knew that they could go on—and so, then, could I.

I was grateful for this understanding and felt that I was allowed to reach it so that my transition through death would be easier.

Now I became filled with the desire to move on with my own life and to experience all that awaited me. I was drawn back to the hospital, but I don't remember the trip; it seemed to happen instantaneously. I saw my body still lying on the bed about two and a half feet below me and slightly to my left. My three friends were still there, waiting for me. Again I felt their love and the joy they felt in helping me.

As I was filled with their love, somehow I knew that it was time for me to move on. I also knew my dear friends, the monks, would not be going with me.

I began to hear a rushing sound.

The Tunnel

When you are in the presence of enormous energy, you know it. I knew it now. A deep rumbling, rushing sound began to fill the room. I sensed the power behind it, a movement that seemed unrelenting. But although the sound and power were awesome, I was filled again with a very pleasant feeling—almost hypnotic. I heard chimes, or distant bells, tinkling in the background—a beautiful sound I'll never forget. Darkness began to surround my being. The bed, the light by the door, the entire room seemed to dim, and immediately I was gently drawn up and into a great, whirling, black mass.

I felt as if I had been swallowed up by an enormous tornado. I could see nothing but the intense, almost tangible darkness. The darkness was more than a lack of light; it was a dense blackness unlike anything I had known before. Common sense told me that I should have been terrified, that all of the fears of my youth should have risen up, but within this black mass I felt a profoundly pleasant sense of well being and calmness. I felt myself moving forward through it, and the whirling sound became fainter. I was in a reclining position, moving feet first, head slightly raised. The speed became so incredible that I felt that light years could not measure it. But the peace and tranquility also increased, and I felt that I could have stayed in this wonderful state forever, and knew that if I wanted to, I could.

I became aware of other people as well as animals traveling with me, but at a distance. I could not see them, but I sensed that their experience was the same as mine. I felt no personal connection to them and knew that they represented no threat to me, so I soon lost awareness of them. I did sense, however, that there were some who were not moving forward as I, but were lingering in this wonderful blackness. They either didn't have the desire, or simply didn't know how to proceed. But there was no fear.

I felt a process of healing take place. Love filled this whirling, moving mass, and I sank more deeply into its warmth and blackness and rejoiced in my security and peace. I thought, "This must be where the valley of the shadow of death is."

I had never felt greater tranquility in my life.

Embraced by the Light

I saw a pinpoint of light in the distance. The black mass around me began to take on more of the shape of a tunnel, and I felt myself traveling through it at an even greater speed, rushing toward the light. I was instinctively attracted to it, although again, I felt that others might not be. As I approached it, I noticed the figure of a man standing in it, with the light radiating all around him. As I got closer the light became brilliant—brilliant beyond any description, far more brilliant than the sun—and I knew that no earthly eyes in their natural state could look upon this light without being destroyed. Only spiritual eyes could endure it—and appreciate it. As I drew closer I began to stand upright.

I saw that the light immediately around him was golden, as if his whole body had a golden halo around it, and I could see that the golden halo burst out from around him and spread into a brilliant, magnificent whiteness that extended out for some distance. I felt his light blending into mine, literally, and I felt my light being drawn to his. It was as if there were two lamps in a room, both shining, their light merging together. It's hard to tell where one light ends and the other begins; they just become one light. Although his light was much brighter than my own, I was aware that my light, too, illuminated us. And as our lights merged, I felt as if I had stepped into his countenance, and I felt an utter explosion of love.

It was the most unconditional love I have ever felt, and as I saw his arms open to receive me I went to him and received his complete embrace and said over and over, "I'm home. I'm home. I'm finally home." I felt his enormous spirit and knew that I had always been a part of him, that in reality I had never been away from him. And I knew that I was worthy to be with him, to embrace him. I knew that he was aware of all my sins and faults, but that they didn't matter right now. He just wanted to hold me and share his love with me, and I wanted to share mine with him.

There was no questioning who he was. I knew that he was my Savior, and friend, and God. He was Jesus Christ, who had always loved me, even when I thought he hated me. He was life itself, love itself, and his love gave me a fullness of joy, even to overflowing. I knew that I had known him from the beginning, from long before my earth life, because my spirit *remembered* him.

All my life I had feared him, and I now saw—I *knew*—that he was my choicest friend. Gently, he opened his arms and let me stand back far enough to look into his eyes, and he said, "Your death was premature, it is not yet your time." No words ever spoken have penetrated me more than these. Until then, I had felt no purpose in life; I had simply ambled along looking for love and goodness but never really knowing if my actions were right. Now, within his words, I felt a mission, a purpose; I didn't know what it was, but I knew that my life on earth had not been meaningless.

It was not yet my time.

My time would come when my mission, my purpose, my *meaning* in this life was accomplished. I had a reason for existing on earth. But even though I understood this, my spirit rebelled. Did this mean I would have to go back? I said to him, "No, I can never leave you now."

He understood what I meant, and his love and acceptance for me never wavered. My thoughts raced on: "Is this Jesus, God, the being I feared all my life? He is nothing like what I had thought. He is filled with love."

Then questions began coming to my mind. I wanted to know why I had died as I had—not prematurely, but how my spirit had come to him before the resurrection. I was still laboring under the teachings and beliefs of my childhood. His light now began to fill my mind, and my questions were answered even before I fully asked them. His light was knowledge. It had power to fill me with all truth. As I gained confidence and let the light flow into me, my questions came faster than I thought possible, and they were just as quickly answered. And the answers were absolute and complete. In my fears, I had misinterpreted death, had expected something that was not so. The grave was never intended for the spirit—only for the body. I felt no judgment for having been mistaken. There was just a feeling that a simple, living truth had replaced my error. I understood that he was the Son of God, though he himself was also a God, and that he had chosen from before the creation of the world to be our Savior. I understood, or rather, I *remembered*, his role as creator of the earth. His mission was to come into the world to teach love. This knowledge was more like remembering. Things were coming back to me from long before my life on earth, things that had been purposely blocked from me by a "veil" of forgetfulness at my birth.

As more questions bubbled out of me, I became aware of his sense of humor. Almost laughing, he suggested that I slow down, that I could know all I desired. But I wanted to know *everything*, from beginning to end. My curiosity had always been a torment to my parents and husband—and sometimes to me—but now it was a blessing, and I was thrilled with the freedom of learning. I was being taught by the master teacher! My comprehension was such that I could understand volumes in an instant. It was as if I could look at a book and comprehend it at a glance—as though I could just sit back while the book revealed itself to me in every detail, forward and backward, inside and out, every nuance and possible suggestion.

All in an instant. As I comprehended one thing, more questions and answers would come to me, all building on each other, and interacting as if all truth were intrinsically connected. The word "omniscient" had never been more meaningful to me. Knowledge permeated me. In a sense it *became* me, and I was amazed at my ability to comprehend the mysteries of the universe simply by reflecting on them.

I wanted to know why there were so many churches in the world. Why didn't God give us only one church, one pure religion? The answer came to me with the purest of understanding. Each of us, I was told, is at a different level of spiritual development and understanding. Each person is therefore prepared for a different level of spiritual knowledge. All religions upon the earth are necessary because there are people who need what they teach. People in one religion may not have a complete understanding of the Lord's gospel and never will have while in that religion. But that religion is used as a stepping stone to further knowledge. Each church fulfills spiritual needs that perhaps others cannot fill. No one church can fulfill everybody's needs at every level. As an individual raises his level of understanding about God and his own eternal progress, he might feel discontented with the teachings of his present church and seek a different philosophy or religion to fill that void. When this occurs he has reached another level of understanding and will long for further truth and knowledge, and for another opportunity to grow. And at every step of the way, these new opportunities to learn will be given.

Having received this knowledge, I knew that we have no right to criticize any church or religion in any way. They are all precious and important in his sight. Very special people with important missions have been placed in all countries, in all religions, in every station of life, that they might touch others. There *is* a fullness of the gospel, but most people will not attain it here. In order to grasp this truth, we need to listen to the Spirit and let go of our egos.

I wanted to learn the purpose of life on the earth. Why are we here? As I basked in the love of Jesus Christ, I couldn't imagine why any spirit would voluntarily leave this wonderful paradise and all it offered—worlds to explore and ideas to create and knowledge to gain. Why would anyone want to come here? In answer, I *remembered* the creation of the earth. I actually experienced it as if it were being re-enacted before my eyes. This was important. Jesus wanted me to internalize this knowledge. He wanted me to know how I felt when the creation occurred. And the only way to do that was for me to view it again and *feel* what I had felt before.

All people as spirits in the pre-mortal world took part in the creation of the earth. We were thrilled to be part of it. We were with God, and we knew that he created us, that we were his very own children. He was pleased with our development and was filled with absolute love for each one of us. Also, Jesus Christ was there. I understood, to my surprise, that Jesus was a separate being from God, with his own divine purpose, and I knew that God was our mutual Father. My Protestant upbringing had taught me that God the Father and Jesus Christ were one being. As we all assembled, the Father explained that coming to earth for a time would further our spiritual growth. Each spirit who was to come to earth assisted in planning the conditions on earth, including the laws of mortality which would govern us. These included the laws of physics as we know them, the limitations of our bodies, and spiritual powers that we would be able to access. We assisted God in the development of plants and animal life that would be here. Everything was created of spirit matter before it was created physically—solar systems, suns, moons, stars, planets, life upon the planets, mountains, rivers, seas, etc. I saw this process, and then, to further understand it, I was told by the Savior that the spirit creation could be compared to one of our photographic prints; the spirit creation would be like a sharp, brilliant print, and the earth would be like its dark negative. This earth is only a shadow of the beauty and glory of its spirit creation, but it is what we needed for our growth. It was important that I understand that we all assisted in creating our conditions here.

Many times the creative thoughts we have in this life are the result of unseen inspiration. Many of our important inventions and even technological developments were first created in the spirit by spirit prodigies. Then individuals on earth received the inspiration to create these inventions here. I understood that there is a vital, dynamic link between the spirit world and mortality, and that we need the spirits on the other side for our progression. I also saw that they are *very* happy to assist us in any way they can.

I saw that in the pre-mortal world we knew about and even chose our missions in life. I understood that our stations in life are based upon the objectives of those missions. Through divine knowledge we knew what many of our tests and experiences would be, and we prepared accordingly. We bonded with others—family members and friends—to help us complete our missions. We needed their help. We came as volunteers, each eager to learn and experience all that God had created for us. I knew that each of us who made the decision to come here was a valiant spirit. Even the least developed among us here was strong and valiant there.

We were given agency to act for ourselves here. Our own actions determine the course of our lives, and we can alter or redirect our lives at any time. I understood that this was crucial; God made the promise that he wouldn't intervene in our lives *unless we asked him*. And then through his omniscient knowledge he would help us attain our righteous desires. We were grateful for this ability to express our free will and to exercise its power. This would allow each of us to obtain great joy or to choose that which will bring us sadness. The choice would be ours through our decisions.

I was actually relieved to find that the earth is not our natural home, that we did not originate here. I was gratified to see that the earth is only a temporary place for our schooling and that sin is not our true nature. Spiritually, we are at various degrees of light—which is knowledge—and because of our divine, spiritual nature we are filled with the desire to do good. Our earthly selves, however, are constantly in opposition to our spirits. I saw how weak the flesh is. But it is persistent. Although our spirit bodies are full of light, truth, and love, they must battle constantly to overcome the flesh, and this strengthens them. Those who are truly developed will find a perfect harmony between their flesh and spirits, a harmony that will bless them with peace and give them the ability to help others.

As we learn to abide by the laws of this creation, we learn how to use those laws to our own good. We learn how to live in harmony with the creative powers around us. God has given us individual talents, some more and some less according to our needs. As we use these talents, we learn how to work with, and eventually understand, the laws and overcome the limitations of this life. By understanding these laws we are better able to serve those around us. Whatever we become here in mortality is meaningless unless it is done for the benefit of others. Our gifts and talents are given to us to help us serve. And in serving others we grow spiritually.

Above all, I was shown that love is supreme. I saw that truly without love we are nothing. We are here to help each other, to care for each other, to understand, forgive, and serve one another. We are here to have love for every person born on earth. Their earthly form might be black, yellow, brown, handsome, ugly, thin, fat, wealthy, poor, intelligent, or ignorant, but we are not to judge by these appearances. Each spirit has the capacity to be filled with love and eternal energy. At the beginning, each possesses some degree of light and truth that can be more fully developed. We cannot measure these things. Only God knows the heart of man, and only God can judge perfectly. He knows our spirits; we see only temporary strengths and weaknesses. Because of our own limitations, we can seldom look into the heart of man.

I knew that anything we do to show love is worthwhile: a smile, a word of encouragement, a small act of sacrifice. We grow by these actions. Not all people are lovable, but when we find someone difficult for us to love, it is often because they remind us of something within ourselves that we don't like. I learned that we must love our enemies—let go of anger, hate, envy, bitterness, and the refusal to forgive. These things destroy the spirit. We will have to account for how we treat others.

Upon receiving the plan of creation, we sang in rejoicing and were filled with God's love. We were filled with joy as we saw the growth we would have here on earth and the joyous bonds we would create with each other.

Then we watched as the earth was created. We watched as our spirit brothers and sisters entered physical bodies for their turns upon the earth, each experiencing the pains and joys that would help them progress. I distinctly remember watching the American pioneers crossing the continent and rejoicing as they endured their difficult tasks and completed their missions. I knew that only those who needed that experience were placed there. I saw the angels rejoicing for those who endured their trials and succeeded and grieving for those who failed. I saw that some failed because of their own weaknesses, and some failed because of the weaknesses of others. I sensed that many of us who were not there would not have been up to the tasks, that we would have made lousy pioneers, and we would have been the cause of more suffering for others. Likewise, some of the pioneers and people from other eras could not have endured the trials of today. We are where we need to be.

As all of these things came to me, I understood the perfection of the plan. I saw that we all volunteered for our positions and stations in the world, and that each of us is receiving more help than we know. I saw the unconditional love of God, beyond any earthly love, radiating from him to all his children. I saw the angels standing near us, waiting to assist us, rejoicing in our accomplishments and joys. But above all, I saw Christ, the Creator and Savior of the earth, my friend, and the closest friend any of us can have. I seemed to melt with joy as I was held in his arms and comforted—home at last. I would give all in my power, all that I ever was, to be filled with that love again—to be embraced in the arms of his eternal light.

The Laws

I was still in the presence of the Lord, with the warmth of his light still bathing me. I was not aware of being in any particular place, of the space around us or of other beings. He saw all that I saw; indeed, he gave me all that I saw and understood.

I remained in his light, and the questions and answers continued. The dialogue between us had actually increased in speed and breadth until it seemed that every facet of existence could be covered. My mind turned again to the laws that govern us here, and his knowledge began pouring into me. I felt a distinct happiness on his part, a pleasure to share this with me.

The Laws

I saw that there are many laws by which we are governed—spiritual laws, physical laws, and universal laws—most of which we have only an inkling. These laws were created to fulfill a purpose, and all laws complement each other. When we recognize these laws and learn how to use their positive and negative forces, we will have access to power beyond comprehension. When we break one of these laws, going against that which is the natural order, we have sinned.

I saw that all things were created by spiritual power. Each element, each particle of creation, has intelligence in it, which intelligence is filled with spirit and life, and thus has the capacity for experiencing joy. Each element is independent to act on its own, to respond to the laws and forces around it; when God speaks to these elements, they respond, and they have joy in obeying his word. It is through the natural powers and laws of creation that Christ created the earth.

I understood that by living true to the laws that govern us we will be further blessed and will receive still greater knowledge. But I also understood that breaking these laws, "sinning," will weaken and possibly destroy all that we have achieved up to that time. There is a cause and effect relationship to sin. We create many of our own punishments through the actions we commit. If we pollute the environment, for example, this is a "sin" against the earth, and we reap the natural consequences of breaking the laws of life. We may be weakened physically or die, or we may cause others to weaken physically or die because of our actions. There are also sins against the flesh, such as over-eating or under-eating, lack of exercise, drug abuse (which includes using *any* substance not in harmony with the organization of our bodies), and other physically debilitating actions. No one of these "sins" of the flesh is greater than another. We are responsible for our bodies.

I saw that each spirit is given ownership of its flesh. While we live in mortality our spirit is to control the body, bringing its appetites and passions into subjection. Everything from within the spirit is manifested in the flesh, but the flesh and attributes of the flesh cannot invade the spirit against the will of the spirit—it is the spirit within us that chooses. It is the spirit which governs. To become as perfect as a mortal being can become, we need to bring the mind, body, and spirit into total harmony. To become perfect in the spirit, we must add to that harmony Christlike love and righteousness.

My whole spirit wanted to shout for joy as these truths came to me. I understood them, and Jesus knew that I was comprehending all that he showed me. My spiritual eyes were opened once again, and I saw that God had created many universes and that within them he controls the elements. He has authority over all laws and energy and matter. Within our universe are both positive and negative energies, and both types of energy are essential to creation and growth. These energies have intelligence—they do our will. They are willing servants. God has absolute power over both energies. Positive energy is basically just what we would think it is: light, goodness, kindness, love, patience, charity, hope, and so on. And negative energy is just what we would think it is: darkness, hatred, fear (Satan's greatest tool), unkindness, intolerance, selfishness, despair, discouragement, and so on.

Positive and negative energies work in opposition to each other. And when we internalize these energies, they become our servants. Positive attracts positive, and negative attracts negative. Light cleaves to light, and darkness loves darkness. If we become mostly positive or mostly negative, we begin to associate with others like us. But *we* have the choice to become positive or negative. Simply by thinking positive thoughts and speaking positive words we attract positive energy. I saw that this is the case. I saw different energies surround different people. I saw how a person's words actually affect the energy field around him. The very *words* themselves—the vibrations in the air—attract one type of energy or another. A person's desires have a similar effect. There is power in our thoughts. We create our own surroundings by the thoughts we think. Physically, this may take a period of time, but spiritually it is instantaneous. If we understood the power of our thoughts, we would guard them more closely. If we understood the awesome power of our words, we would prefer silence to almost anything negative. In our thoughts and words we create our own weaknesses and our own strengths. Our limitations and joys begin in our hearts. We can always replace negative with positive.

Because our thoughts can affect this eternal energy, they are the source of creation. All creation begins in the mind. It must be *thought* first. Gifted people are able to use their imaginations to create new things; both wonderful and terrible. Some people come to this earth with their powers of imagination already well developed, and I saw that some of them misuse that power here. Some people use negative energy to create harmful things—items or words that can destroy. Others use their imaginations in positive ways, to the betterment of those around them. These people truly create joy and are blessed. There is a literal power in the creations of the mind. Thoughts are deeds.

I understood that life is lived most fully in the imagination—that, ironically, imagination is the key to reality. This is something I never would have supposed. We are sent here to live life fully, to live it *abundantly*, to find joy in our own creations, whether they are new thoughts or *things* or emotions or experiences. We are to create our own lives, to exercise our gifts and experience both failure and success. We are to use our free will to expand and magnify our lives.

With all of this understanding, I understood again that love is supreme. Love must govern. Love always governs the spirit, and the spirit must be strengthened to rule the mind and flesh. I understood the natural order of love everywhere. First, we must love the Creator. This is the greatest love we can have (although we may not know this until we meet him). Then we must love ourselves. I knew that without feelings of self-love that the love we feel for others is counterfeit. Then, we must love *all* others as ourselves. As we see the light of Christ in ourselves, we will see it in others too, and it will become impossible not to love that part of God in them.

As I remained in the Savior's glow, in his absolute love, I realized that when I had feared him as a child I had actually moved myself further from him. When I thought he didn't love me, I was moving my love from him. He never moved. I saw now that he was like a sun in my galaxy. I moved all around him, sometimes nearer and sometimes farther away, but his love never failed.

I understood how others had been instrumental in distancing me from him, though I felt no bitterness or judgment toward them. I saw how men and women in authority over me had become prey to negative energy and had taught belief in God through fear. Their aims were positive, but their deeds were negative. Because of their own fears, they were using fear to control others. They intimidated those under them to believe in God, to "fear God or go to hell."

This prevented me from really loving God. I understood again that fear is the opposite of love and is Satan's greatest tool. Since I feared God, I could not truly love him, and in not loving him, I couldn't love myself or others purely either. The law of love had been broken.

Christ continued to smile upon me. He was pleased with my pleasure in learning, with my excitement in the experience.

Now I knew that there actually was a God. No longer did I believe in just a Universal Power, but now I saw the Man behind that Power. I saw a loving Being who created the universe and placed all knowledge within it. I saw that he governs this knowledge and controls its power. I understood with pure knowledge that God wants us to become as he is, and that he has invested us with god-like qualities, such as the power of imagination and creation, free will, intelligence, and most of all, the power to love. I understood that he actually *wants* us to draw on the powers of heaven, and that by *believing* that we are capable of doing so, we can.

Healing—and Dying

*T*his flow of understanding progressed naturally in the presence of the Savior, from point to point, each element of truth progressing inevitably into the next. After learning of the two major energy forces in the universe, both subject to the authority of God, I saw how these powers can affect us physically. Remembering that the spirit and the mind have tremendous influence on the flesh, I saw that we literally have power to affect our own health. I saw that the spirit in each of us is powerful, that it can give strength to the body to ward off illness, or, once the body is sick, to cause it to heal. The spirit has power to control the mind, and the mind controls the body. Often in reflecting on this principle I have been reminded of the scripture: "For as [a man] thinketh in his heart, so is he" (Proverbs 23:7).

Our thoughts have exceptional power to draw on the negative or positive energies around us. When they draw at length on the negative, the result can be a weakening of the body's defenses. This is especially true when our negative thoughts are centered on ourselves. I understood that we are at our *most* self-centered state when we are depressed. Nothing can sap our natural strength and health as much as prolonged depression. But when we make the effort to move ourselves away from self and begin to concentrate on the needs of others and how to serve them, we begin to heal. Service is a balm to both the spirit and body.

All healing takes place from within. Our spirits heal our body. A doctor's sure hands may perform surgery, and medicine may provide ideal circumstances for health, but it is the spirit then that effects the healing. A body without a spirit cannot be healed; it cannot live for long. I was shown that the cells of our bodies were engineered to provide life indefinitely. They were programmed in the beginning to regenerate themselves, to replace old cells that had become ineffective or damaged so that life would not end. But something changed this; I was not shown exactly what the process was, but I understood that "death" had entered mortality in the Garden of Eden. I was shown that there *was* a Garden of Eden, and I was shown that decisions there created conditions that make eternal life in mortality impossible.

Our bodies *must* die, but there is still the power within us, using faith and positive energy, to alter our cells so that we can be healed—if it is right. We must remember that God's will is always involved with healing.

I was shown that many of the illnesses of my life were the result of depression or feelings of not being loved. I saw that I had often yielded to negative "self-talk," such as "Oh, my aches and pains," "I'm not loved," "Look at my sufferings," "I can't endure this," and more. Suddenly I saw the *me, me, me* in each of these statements. I saw the extent of my self-centered-ness. And I saw that not only did I claim these negativisms by calling them mine, but I opened the door and accepted them as mine. My body then lived a sort of self-fulfilling prophecy: "Woe is me," was translated in the body as "I am sick." I had never thought of this before, but now I saw how clearly I had been a part of the problem.

I understood that positive self-talk begins the healing process. Once we have identified the illness or problem, we need to start verbalizing its remedy. We need to remove thoughts of the illness from our minds and begin concentrating on its cure. Then we need to verbalize this cure, letting our words add to the power of our thoughts. This creates an excitement in the intelligences around us, and they then go into motion, working to heal us. I understood that this verbalization can best be done in prayer. If it is right that we be healed, God will then assist us in the healing process.

We are not to deny the presence of the illness or problem, we are simply to deny its power over our divine right to remove it. We are to live by faith, not by sight. Sight is involved with the cognitive, the analytical mind. It rationalizes and justifies. Faith is governed by the spirit. The spirit is emotional, accepting, and internalizes. And, as with every other attribute, the way to gain faith is to practice the use of it. If we learn to use what we have, we will receive more. This is a spiritual law.

Developing faith is like planting seeds. Even if some of our seeds fall by the wayside, we will still receive some harvest. *Any* act of faith will bless us.

And, the more proficient we become (and we will become proficient if we practice), the greater our harvest of faith will be. Everything produces after its own kind. This too is a spiritual law.

Now I was truly beginning to understand the power of the spirit over the body, and I saw that the spirit functions at a level most of us are not aware of. Of course I knew that my mind created my thoughts, and my body performed my actions, but the spirit had been a mystery to me. Now I understood that the spirit is a mystery to most people. I saw that it functions, generally, without the mind even being aware of it. The spirit communicates with God, being the receptive device that receives knowledge and insight from him. It was important for me to understand this, and I envisioned that this would appear much like a fluorescent light tube in our bodies. When the light is glowing, our core is filled with light and love; it is this energy that gives the body life and power. I saw also that the light could be diminished and the spirit weakened through negative experience—through lack of love, through violence, sexual abuse, or other damaging experiences. By weakening the spirit, these experiences also weaken the body. The body may not get sick, but it is more susceptible then, until the spirit is recharged. We can recharge our own spirits through serving others, having faith in God, and simply opening ourselves to positive energy through positive thoughts. *We* control it. The source of energy is God and is always there, but we must tune him in. We must accept the power of God if we want to enjoy the effects of it in our lives.

To my surprise I saw that most of us had selected the illnesses we would suffer, and for some, the illness that would end our lives. Sometimes healing does not come immediately, or at all, because of our need for growth. All experience is for our good, and sometimes it takes what we would consider negative experience to help develop our spirits. We were very willing, even anxious, as spirits to accept all of our ailments, illnesses, and accidents here to help better ourselves spiritually. I understood that in the spirit world our earth time is meaningless. The pain we experience on earth is just a moment, just a split second of consciousness in the spirit world, and we are very willing to endure it. Our deaths are also often calculated to help us grow. When a person dies of cancer, for example, he will often experience a long, painful death that may give him opportunities for growth that he cannot get otherwise. I knew that my mother had died of cancer, and I understood that she was able to interact with her family members toward the end in ways she hadn't before. Relationships were improved, and healed. She had grown as a result of her death. Some people choose to die in ways that will help someone else.

A person may have chosen to die, for example, by stepping into the street and being hit by a drunk driver. This seems terrible to us, but within the pure knowledge of God, his spirit knew that he was actually saving this driver more grief later. The driver may have been drunk again a week later and hit a group of teenagers, maiming them or causing greater pain and misery than was necessary, but he was prevented because he was spending time in jail for hitting the person who had already completed his purpose on earth. In the eternal perspective, unnecessary pain was spared for the young people, and a growing experience may have begun for the driver.

There are far fewer accidents here than we imagine, especially in things that affect us eternally. The hand of God, and the path we chose before we came here, guide many of our decisions and even many of the seemingly random experiences we have. It's fruitless to try to identify them all, but they do happen, and for a purpose. Even experiences such as divorce, sudden unemployment, or being victim of violence may ultimately give us knowledge and contribute to our spiritual development. Although these experiences are painful, they can help us grow. As Jesus said while in his earthly ministry, " . . . for it must needs be that offences come; but woe to that man by whom the offence cometh!" (Matt. 18:7.)

Under the guidance of the Savior I learned that it was important for me to accept all experience as potentially good. I needed to accept my purpose and station in life. I could take the negative things that had happened to me and try to overcome their effects. I could forgive my enemies, even love them, and thereby nullify any bad influence they may have had on me. I could seek good thoughts and kind words, and thus bring healing ointment to my own soul, as well as to others. I saw that I could begin to heal myself, spiritually first, then emotionally, mentally, and physically. I saw that I could spare myself the corrosive effects of despair. I had a right to live fully.

I saw the evil in surrendering to one of Satan's greatest tools—my personal cycles of guilt and fear. I understood that I had to let go of the past. If I had broken laws or sinned, I needed to change my heart, forgive myself, and then move onward. If I had hurt someone, I needed to start loving them—honestly— and seek their forgiveness. If I had damaged my own spirit, I needed to approach God and feel his love again—his healing love. Repentance can be as easy as we make it—or as difficult. When we fall down, we need to get up, dust ourselves off, and get moving again. If we fall down again, even a million times, we still need to keep going; we're growing more than we think. In the spirit world they don't see sin as we do here. *All* experiences can be positive. All are learning experiences.

We must never consider suicide. This act will only cause us to lose opportunities for further development while here on earth. And afterwards, in reflecting back on these lost opportunities we would feel much pain and sorrow. It is important to remember, though, that God is the judge of each soul and the severity of each soul's trials. Seek hope, in at least one positive act, and you may begin to see a glimmer of light that you had missed before. Despair is *never* justified, because it is never needed. We are here to learn, to experiment, to make mistakes. We don't need to judge ourselves harshly; we just need to take life one step at a time, not worrying about other people's judgment of us, nor measuring ourselves by their measuring sticks. We need to forgive ourselves and be grateful for the things that help us grow. Our most severe challenges will one day reveal themselves to be our greatest teachers.

Because I knew that all creation begins with thoughts, I also knew that the creation of sin, and of guilt, and of despair, and of hope, and of love all start within us. All healing comes from within. All misery comes from within. We can create our own spiral of despair, or we can create a trampoline of happiness and attainment. Our thoughts have *tremendous* power.

We are like babies crawling around, trying to learn how to use the forces within us. They are powerful forces and are governed by laws that will protect us from ourselves. But as we grow and seek the positive all around us, even the laws themselves will be revealed. We will be given all that we are prepared to receive.

The Looms and the Library

*T*hrough receiving this information, I developed a relationship and knowledge of the Savior that I will always cherish. His concern for my feelings was inspiring; he never wanted to do or say anything that would offend me. He knew what I was capable of understanding and he carefully prepared me to absorb all of the knowledge that I sought. In the spirit world no one is made to feel uncomfortable by being forced to do or accept things for which they are not prepared. Patience is a natural attribute there.

I'll never forget the Lord's sense of humor, which was as delightful and quick as any here—far more so. Nobody could out-do his humor. He is filled with perfect happiness, perfect goodwill. There is a softness and grace in his presence, and I had no doubt that he is a perfect man. I *knew* him, his spirit, his feelings, his concern for me. I felt his kinship with me, and I knew that we were family. I felt that his relationship to me was both like a father and an older brother. He was close to me, but there was also an element of authority. He was tender and good natured, but also responsible. I knew with a sure knowledge that he would never misuse his authority, that he would never even desire to do so.

Still surrounded by light, Jesus smiled at me, and I felt his approval. He turned to his left and introduced me to two women who had just appeared. A third woman also appeared briefly behind them, but she appeared to be on an errand and only stopped to visit for a moment. Jesus instructed the first two women to escort me, and I felt their happiness at being with me. As I looked at them, I remembered them; they were my friends! They had been two of my close friends before I came to earth, and their excitement at being with me again was as great as my own. As Jesus was about to leave me with them, I felt his amusement again, and he seemed to whisper to my spirit, "Go learn of things," and I understood that I was free to see and experience all that I wanted. I was thrilled that there was still more to learn—much more as it would turn out. The Savior left us then, and my two friends embraced me. The love here encompassed all; everybody had it. Everybody was happy. Although there was a vast difference in the light and power between these women and Christ, their love was unconditional. They loved me with all of their hearts.

The memory of that tour has been partially taken from me. I remember being taken into a large room where people were working, but I don't remember how we got there or what the building looked like from the outside. The room was beautiful. Its walls were made of some kind of substance, perhaps like a very thin marble, that let light come in, and in places I could see through it to the outside. The effect was very interesting and beautiful.

As we approached the people, I saw that they were weaving on large, ancient-looking looms. My first impression was "how archaic" to have manual looms in the spirit world. Standing by the looms were many spiritual beings, male and female, and they greeted me with smiles. They were delighted to see me and moved back from one of the looms to let me have a better look. They were anxious for me to see the workmanship of their hands. I went closer and picked up a piece of the cloth that they were weaving. Its appearance was like a mixture of spun glass and spun sugar. As I moved the cloth back and forth, it shimmered and sparkled, almost as though it were alive. The effect was startling. The material was opaque on one side, but when I turned it over I was able to see through it. Being transparent from one side and opaque on the other—similar to a two-way mirror—obviously had a purpose, but I wasn't told what the purpose was. The workers explained that the material would be made into clothing for those coming into the spirit world from earth. The workers were understandably pleased with their work and with my gratitude for being permitted to see it.

We moved from the looms, my two companions and I, and went through many other rooms where I saw amazing things and wonderful people, but I have not been allowed to recall many of these details. I remember the feeling of traveling for days or weeks and never tiring. I was surprised at how much people like to work with their hands there—those who want to. They enjoy creating devices that are helpful to others—both here and there. I saw a large machine, similar to a computer, but much more elaborate and powerful. The people working on this too were pleased to show me their work. Again, I understood that all things of importance are created spiritually first and physically second. I had no idea of this before.

I was taken to another large room similar to a library. As I looked around it seemed to be a repository of knowledge, but I couldn't see any books. Then I noticed ideas coming into my mind, knowledge filling me on subjects that I had not thought about for some time—or in some cases not at all. Then I realized that this was a library of the mind. By simply reflecting on a topic, as I had earlier in Christ's presence, all knowledge on that topic came to me. I could learn about anybody in history—or even in the spirit world—in full detail.

No knowledge was kept from me, and it was impossible not to understand correctly every thought, every statement, every particle of knowledge. There was absolutely no misunderstanding here. History was pure. Understanding was complete. I understood not only what people did but why they did it and how it affected other people's perceptions of reality. I understood reality pertaining to that subject from every angle, from every possible perception; and all of this brought a wholeness to an event or person or principle that was not possible to comprehend on earth.

But this was more than a mental process. I was able to *feel* what the people felt when they performed these actions. I understood their pains or joys or excitement because I was able to live them. Some of this knowledge was taken from me, but not all. I cherish the knowledge granted me of certain events and people in our history which were important for me to understand.

I wanted still more experiences in this wonderful, incredible world, and my escorts were delighted to continue helping me. It was their greatest joy to give me joy, and with some excitement they took me outside to a garden.

The Garden

*A*s we went outdoors into the garden I saw mountains, spectacular valleys, and rivers in the distance. My escorts left me, and I was allowed to proceed alone, perhaps to experience the full beauty of the garden unencumbered by the presence of others. The garden was filled with trees and flowers and plants that somehow made their setting seem inevitable, as if they were *meant* to be exactly how and where they were. I walked on the grass for a time. It was crisp, cool, and brilliant green, and it felt alive under my feet. But what filled me with awe in the garden more than anything were the intense colors. We have nothing like them.

When light strikes an object here, the light reflects off that object in a certain color. Thousands of shades are possible. Light in the spirit world doesn't necessarily reflect off anything. It comes from within and appears to be a living essence. A million, a billion colors are possible.

The flowers, for example, are so vivid and luminescent with color that they don't seem to be solid. Because of each plant's intense aura of light, it is difficult to define where the plant's surface starts and stops. It is obvious that each part of the plant, each microscopic part, is made up of its own intelligence. This is the best word I can use to define it. Every minute part is filled with its own life and can be reorganized with other elements to create anything in existence. The same element that now resides in a flower may later be part of something else—and just as alive. It doesn't have a spirit as we do, but it has intelligence and organization and can react to the will of God and other universal laws. All of this is evident as you see creation there, and particularly evident in the flowers.

A beautiful river ran through the garden not far from me, and I was immediately drawn to it. I saw that the river was fed by a large cascading waterfall of the purest water, and from there the river fed into a pond. The water dazzled with its clarity and life.

Life. It was in the water too. Each drop from the waterfall had its own intelligence and purpose. A melody of majestic beauty carried from the waterfall and filled the garden, eventually merging with other melodies that I was now only faintly aware of. The music came from the water itself, from its intelligence, and each drop produced its own tone and melody which mingled and interacted with every other sound and strain around it. The water was praising God for its life and joy. The overall effect seemed beyond the ability of any symphony or composer here. In comparison, our best music here would sound like a child playing a tin drum. We simply don't have the capacity to comprehend the vastness and strength of the music there, let alone begin to create it. As I got closer to the water the thought came to me that these could possibly be the "living waters" mentioned in the scriptures, and I wanted to bathe in them.

As I approached the water, I noticed a rose near me that seemed to stand out from the other flowers, and I stopped to examine it. Its beauty was breathtaking. Among all the flowers there, none captured me like this one. It was gently swaying to faint music, and singing praises to the Lord with sweet tones of its own. I realized that I could actually see it growing. As it developed before my eyes, my spirit was moved, and I wanted to experience its life, to step into it and feel its spirit. As this thought came to me, I seemed to be able to see down into it. It was as though my vision had become microscopic and allowed me to penetrate the rose's deepest parts. But it was much more than a visual experience. I felt the rose's presence around me, as if I were actually inside and part of the flower. I experienced it as if I *were* the flower. I felt the rose swaying to the music of all the other flowers, and I felt it creating its own music, a melody that perfectly harmonized with the thousands of other roses joining it. I understood that the music in my flower came from its individual parts, that its petals produced their own tones, and that each intelligence within that petal was adding to its perfect notes, each working harmoniously for the overall effect—which was joy. My joy was absolutely full again! I felt God in the plant, in me, his love pouring into us. We were all one!

I will never forget the rose that I was. That one experience, just a glimmer of the grander joy that is available in the spirit world, in being one with everything else, was so great that I will cherish it forever.

The Greeting Party

*I*nto the garden came a group of spiritual beings. Many were wearing soft pastel gowns now, reflecting, perhaps, the spirit of the location as well as the occasion. They surrounded me, and I felt that they were gathering to celebrate a sort of graduation party for me. I had died (or graduated, as their term seemed to indicate), and they were there to greet me. Their faces were beaming with delight as though they were looking at a child who had just enjoyed something incredibly delicious for the first time. I realized that I remembered them all from before my earth life, and I ran to them and hugged and kissed each one. My ministering angels—my dear monks—were there again, and I kissed them.

As I felt each of their spirits, I realized that they were there to support me. My escorts, who continued to act as my guides, now told me that I had died prematurely and that this wasn't really a graduation party, but a time to show me what I would receive when I returned at the right time. They were very happy to see me and to support me, but they knew I had to go back. Then they explained to me about death.

When we "die," my guides said, we experience nothing more than a transition to another state. Our spirits slip from the body and move to a spiritual realm. If our deaths are traumatic, the spirit quickly leaves the body, sometimes even before death occurs. If a person is in an accident or fire, for example, their spirit may be taken from their body before they experience much pain. The body may actually appear still alive for some moments, but the spirit will have already left and be in a state of peace.

At the time of death, we are given the choice to remain on this earth until our bodies are buried or to move on, as I did, to the level to which our spirit had grown. I understood that there are many levels of development, and we will always go to that level where we are most comfortable. Most spirits choose to remain on earth for a short time and comfort their loved ones; families are subject to much more grief than the departed one. Sometimes the spirits will remain longer if the loved ones are in despair. They remain to help the loved ones' spirits heal.

I also was told that our prayers can benefit both spiritual beings as well as persons on the earth. If there is reason to fear for a departed person's spirit, if there is reason to believe their transition may be difficult or unwanted, we can pray for them and enlist spiritual help.

They told me that it is important for us to acquire knowledge of the spirit while we are in the flesh. The more knowledge we acquire here, the further and faster we will progress there. Because of lack of knowledge or belief, some spirits are virtual prisoners of this earth. Some who die as atheists, or those who have bonded to the world through greed, bodily appetites, or other earthly commitments find it difficult to move on, and they become earth-bound. They often lack the faith and power to reach for, or in some cases even to recognize, the energy and light that pulls us toward God. These spirits stay on the earth until they learn to accept the greater power around them and to let go of the world. When I was in the black mass before moving towards the light, I felt the presence of such lingering spirits. They reside there as long as they want to in its love and warmth, accepting its healing influence, but eventually they learn to move on to accept the greater warmth and security of God.

Of all knowledge, however, there is none more essential than knowing Jesus Christ. I was told that he is the door through which we will *all* return. He is the only door through which we can return. Whether we learn of Jesus Christ here or while in the spirit, we must eventually accept him and surrender to his love.

My friends in the garden were full of love as they stood around me, and they realized that I didn't want to go back yet, that I wanted to see more. In their desire to please me, they showed me *much* more.

Many Worlds

My memory was opened further than before, reaching back beyond the creation of our earth into eternities past. I remembered that God was the creator of many worlds, galaxies, and realms beyond our understanding, and I wanted to see them. As the desire came, my thoughts gave me power, and I drifted away from the garden, escorted this time by two different beings of light who then became my guides. Our spiritual bodies floated away from my friends and into the blackness of space.

Our speed increased, and I felt the exhilaration of flight. I could do whatever I wanted, go wherever I desired, go fast—incredibly fast—or go slow. I loved the freedom. I entered the vastness of space and learned that it is not a void; it was full of love and light—the tangible presence of the Spirit of God. I heard a soft, pleasant sound, a distant but comforting sound that made me happy. It was a tone, similar to a note of music, but was universal and seemed to fill all the space around me. It was followed by another tone at a different pitch, and soon I noticed something of a melody—a vast, cosmic song that soothed and comforted me. The tones produced soft vibrations, and as they touched me I knew that they possessed the power to heal. I knew that anything touched by these tones would receive the effects of their healing; they were like spiritual salve, expressions of love that mended broken spirits. I learned from the escorts traveling with me that not all musical tones are healing—that some can create within us negative emotional responses. I understood now that while I was on earth, Satan had used these negative tones in music which actually produced illness in my mind and body.

Some of the details of what followed have been removed from my memory, but many impressions remain. I seemed to be gone for weeks, even months, visiting the many creations of God. As I traveled, I always felt the comforting presence of God's love. I sensed that I was "back" in my native environment and was doing only that which was natural. I traveled to many other worlds—earths like our own but more glorious, and always filled with loving, intelligent people. We are *all* God's children, and he has filled the immensity of space for us. I traveled tremendous distances, knowing that the stars I saw were not visible from earth. I saw galaxies and traveled to them with ease and almost instantaneous speed, visiting their worlds and meeting more children of our God, all of them our spiritual brothers and sisters. And all of this was a remembering, a reawakening. I knew that I had been to these places before.

Much later, when I returned to my mortal body, I felt cheated when I was unable to remember the details of this experience, but with the passage of time I have learned that I needed this forgetfulness for my own good. If I could remember the glorious and perfect worlds I had seen, I would live a constantly frustrated life and mar my own God-given mission. My feeling of being cheated has given way to a sense of awe and deep gratitude for the experience. God didn't *have* to show me other worlds, and he didn't have to let me remember anything about them. In his mercy, though, he has given me much; I saw worlds that our most powerful telescopes could never see, and I know the love that exists there.

Selecting a Body

I returned to the garden and met my earlier escorts again. I had seen people progressing in the worlds I had visited, working toward becoming more like our Father, and I was curious about our development on earth. How do we grow?

My escorts were pleased with my question, and they took me to a place where many spirits prepared for life on earth. They were mature spirits—I saw no children spirits during my entire experience. I saw how desirous these spirits were of coming to earth. They looked upon life here as a school where they could learn many things and develop the attributes they lacked. I was told that we had all *desired* to come here, that we had actually chosen many of our weaknesses and difficult situations in our lives so that we could grow. I also understood that sometimes we were given weaknesses which would be for our good. The Lord also gives us gifts and talents according to his will. We should never compare our talents or weaknesses to another's. We each have what we need; we are unique. Equality of spiritual weaknesses or gifts is not important.

The area immediately in front of and below me scrolled back, as if a window were opening, and I saw the earth. I saw both the physical world and the spiritual world. I saw that some of the righteous spirit children of our Father in Heaven did not choose to come here to this earth. They have selected to stay as spirits with God and act as guardian angels for people here. I also understood that there are other types of angels, including a type called "Warring Angels." It was shown to me that their purpose is to do battle for us against Satan and his angels. Although we each have protecting, or guardian, spirits to assist us, there are times when the Warring Angels are necessary to protect us, and I understood that they are available to us through prayer. I saw that they are giant men, very muscularly built, with a wonderful countenance about them. They are magnificent spirits. I understood simply by looking at them that to struggle against them would be an act of futility. They were actually dressed like warriors, in head dress and armor, and I saw that they moved more swiftly than other angels. But perhaps what set them apart more than anything was their aura of confidence; they were absolutely sure of their abilities. Nothing evil could daunt them, and they knew it. As they suddenly rushed off on some mission (which was not revealed to me), I was moved by their looks of concern; they understood the importance of their mission, and they knew, and I knew, that they would not return until it was accomplished.

Satan desires to have us, and sometimes when he marshals his forces against one of us that person will need special protection. All of us are always protected, though, by the fact that Satan cannot read our thoughts. He can, however, read our countenances, which can almost be the same as reading our thoughts. Our auras, or countenances, display the feelings and emotions of our souls. God sees them, angels see them, and Satan sees them. Even very sensitive people here can see them. We can protect ourselves by controlling our thoughts, by allowing the light of Christ to enter our lives. As we do this, the light of Christ will shine through us and will actually appear in our countenances.

As I understood this, I saw again the spirits who had not yet come to earth, and I saw some of them hovering over people in mortality. I saw one male spirit trying to get a mortal man and woman together on earth–his future parents. He was playing cupid and was having a very difficult time. The man and woman seemed to want to go in opposite directions and were unwittingly very uncooperative. This male spirit was coaching them, speaking to them, trying to persuade them to get together. Other spirits became concerned as they saw his difficulty, and they took up the cause, several of them trying to "corral" these two young people.

I was told that we had bonded together in the spirit world with certain spirit brothers and sisters–those we felt especially close to. My escorts explained that we covenanted with these spirits to come to earth as family or friends. This spiritual bonding was a result of the love we developed for each other over an eternity of being together. We also chose to come to earth with certain others because of the work we would do together. Some of us wanted to unite in a cause to change certain things on earth, and we could best do it with certain circumstances brought about by selected parents or others. Some of us simply wanted to strengthen a course already set and to pave the way for those who follow. We understood the influences we would have upon each other in this life and the physical and behavioral attributes we would receive from our families. We were aware of the genetic coding of mortal bodies and the particular physical features we would have. We wanted and needed these.

We understood that memories would be contained in the cells of our new bodies. This was an idea that was completely new to me. I learned that all thoughts and experiences in our lives are recorded in our subconscious minds. They are also recorded in our cells, so that, not only is each cell imprinted with a genetic coding, it is also imprinted with every experience we have ever had. Further, I understood that these memories are passed down through the genetic coding to our children. These memories then account for many of the passed on traits in families, such as addictive tendencies, fears, strengths, and so on. I also learned that we do not have repeated lives on this earth; when we seem to "remember" a past life, we are actually recalling memories contained in the cells.

I saw that we understood all the challenges of our complicated physical makeup, and we were confident in accepting these circumstances.

We were also given the spiritual attributes we would need for our missions, many of them specially designed for our needs. Our parents had their own set of spiritual attributes, some of which may have been passed down to us, and we watched how they used these abilities. While maturing, we also acquired other attributes. Now we have our own set of spiritual tools, and we can continue to learn how to use these abilities or we can choose not to use them at all. No matter what our age is, we can continue to acquire new spiritual attributes that can help us in old or new situations. The choice is always there. I saw that we *always* have the right attribute to help ourselves, though we may not have recognized it or learned how to use it. We need to look within. We need to trust our abilities; the right spiritual tool is always there for us.

After watching the spirits trying to corral these two young people together, my attention turned to other spirits making preparations to go to earth. One exceptionally brilliant and dynamic spirit was just entering his mother's womb. He had chosen to enter this world mentally handicapped. He was very excited about this opportunity and was aware of the growth he and his parents would achieve. The three of them had bonded with each other and planned for this arrangement long before. He chose to begin his mortal life at his body's conception, and I watched his spirit move into the womb and enter the newly formed life. He was anxious to feel the great love of his mortal parents.

I learned that spirits can choose to enter their mother's body at any stage of her pregnancy. Once there, they immediately begin experiencing mortality. Abortion, I was told, is contrary to that which is natural. The spirit coming into the body feels a sense of rejection and sorrow. It knows that the body was to be his, whether it was conceived out of wedlock or was handicapped or was only strong enough to live a few hours. But the spirit also feels compassion for its mother, knowing that she made a decision based on the knowledge she had.

I saw many spirits who would only come to the earth for a short time, living only hours, or days after their birth. They were as excited as the others, knowing that they had a purpose to fulfill. I understood that their deaths had been appointed before their births—as were all of ours. These spirits did not need the development that would result from longer lives in mortality, and their deaths would provide challenges that would help their parents grow. The grief that comes here is intense but short. After we are united again, all pain is washed away, and only the joy of our growth and togetherness is felt.

I was surprised at how many plans and decisions were made for the benefit of others. We were all willing to make sacrifices for others. Everything is done for the growth of the spirit—all experience, all gifts and weaknesses are designed for this growth. The things of this world matter little to us there—almost not at all. *Everything* is seen through spiritual eyes.

A time was established for each of us to complete our earthly education. Some spirits would come only to be born, to give experience to others and then pass quickly out of this world. Some would live to an old age to complete their goals and benefit others by allowing them opportunities to serve. Some would come to be our leaders or followers, our soldiers, or our rich or poor, and the purpose for their coming would be to provide situations and relationships that would allow us to learn to love. All who would be led into our paths would lead us to our ultimate achievement. We were to be tested under challenging conditions to see how we would live the most important commandment of all—to love one another. We are *all* collectively bonded to each other while on earth, united in this one supreme purpose—to learn to love one another.

Before this scene of the pre-earth life spirits was closed up, my attention was drawn to another spirit. She was one of the most charming and delightful beings I had seen yet. She was buoyant with energy and radiated a contagious cheer to all around her. Watching her with wonder, I recognized the feeling of a close bond between us and the love that I knew she felt for me. My memory of this moment has been mostly blocked, but I knew that I would never forget her, and there was no doubt that wherever she went she was going to be somebody's special angel.

During this view of the pre-mortal existence, I was impressed by the beauty and glory of each spirit. I knew that I had been there before, that each of us had, and that we had been filled with light and beauty. Then the thought came to me, referring to us all: "If you could see yourself before you were born, you would be amazed at your intelligence and glory. Birth is a sleep and a forgetting."

The Drunken Man

Coming to earth is much like selecting a college and choosing a course of study. We are all at various levels of spiritual development, and we have come here in the stations that best suit our spiritual needs. The minute we judge others for their faults or shortcomings, we are displaying a similar shortcoming in ourselves. We don't have the knowledge to judge people accurately here.

As if to illustrate this principle for me, the heavens scrolled back, and I saw the earth again. This time my vision focused on a street corner in a large city. There, I saw a man lying in a drunken stupor on the sidewalk near a building. One of my guides said, "What do you see?"

The Drunken Man

"Why, a drunken bum lying in his wallow," I said, not understanding why I had to see this.

My guides became excited. They said, "Now we will show you who he really is."

His spirit was revealed to me, and I saw a magnificent man, full of light. Love emanated from his being, and I understood that he was greatly admired in the heavens. This great being came to earth as a teacher to help a friend that he had spiritually bonded with.

His friend was a prominent attorney who had an office a few blocks away from this corner. Although the drunk now had no recollection of this agreement with his friend, his purpose was to be a reminder to him of the needs of others. I understood that the attorney was naturally compassionate, but seeing the drunk would spark him to do more for those who needed his means. I knew that they would see each other, and the attorney would recognize the spirit within the drunk—the man within the man—and be moved to do much good. They would never know their covenanted roles here, but their missions would be fulfilled nonetheless. The drunk had sacrificed his time on earth for the benefit of another. His development would continue and other things he might need for progression would be given him later.

I recollected that I, too, had met people who had seemed familiar to me. The first time I met them I felt an instant closeness, a recognition, but hadn't known why. Now I knew that they had been sent to my path for a reason. They had always been special to me.

My escorts spoke again, bringing me out of my thoughts, and said that because I lacked pure knowledge I should never judge another. Those who passed by the drunk on the corner could not see the noble spirit within, and so judged by outward appearances. I had been guilty of this kind of judgment, silently judging others based on their wealth or outward abilities. I saw now that I had been unjust, that I had no idea of what their lives were like, or, more importantly, what their spirits were like.

The thought also came to me, "For ye have the poor with you always, and whensoever ye will ye may do them good." But even as this scripture came to me it bothered me. Why do we have the poor with us? Why couldn't the Lord provide everything? Why couldn't he just prompt the attorney to share his money with others? The guides broke into my thoughts again and said, "There are angels that walk among you, that you are unaware of."

I was puzzled. The guides then helped me to understand. We *all* have needs, not just the poor. And all of us have made commitments in the spirit world to help each other. But we are slow to keep our covenants made so long ago. So the Lord sends angels to prompt us, to help us be true to these obligations. He won't force us, but he can prompt us. We don't know who these beings are—they appear like anybody else—but they are with us more often than we know.

I didn't feel rebuked, but I knew I had clearly misunderstood—and underestimated—the Lord's help for us here. He will give us all the help he can without interfering in our personal agency and free will. We must be willing to help each other. We must be willing to see that the poor are as worthy of our esteem as the rich. We must be willing to accept *all* others, even those different from us. All are worthy of our love and kindness. We have no right to be intolerant or angry or "fed up." We have no right to look down at others or condemn them in our hearts. The only thing we can take with us from this life is the good that we have done to others. I saw that all of our good deeds and kind words will come back to bless us a hundred fold after this life. Our strength will be found in our charity.

My escorts and I were silent a moment. The drunk was gone from my sight. My soul was filled with understanding and love. Oh, that I could help others as that drunk will help his friend. Oh, that I could be a blessing to others in my life. My soul reverberated with the final fact: Our strength will be found in our charity.

Prayer

I was humbled by the knowledge pouring into me about humanity, about the heavenly worth of each soul. I hungered for more light and knowledge. The heavens scrolled back again, and I saw the sphere of earth rotating in space. I saw many lights shooting up from the earth like beacons. Some were very broad and charged into heaven like broad laser beams. Others resembled the illumination of small pen lights, and some were mere sparks. I was surprised as I was told that these beams of power were the prayers of people on earth.

I saw angels rushing to answer the prayers. They were organized to give as much help as possible. As they worked within this organization, they literally flew from person to person, from prayer to prayer, and were filled with love and joy by their work. They delighted to help us and were especially joyful when somebody prayed with enough intensity and faith to be answered immediately. They always responded to the brighter, larger prayers first, then each prayer in turn, until all of them were answered. I did notice, however, that insincere prayers of repetition have little if any light; and having no power, many of them are not heard.

I was distinctly told that *all* prayers of desire are heard and answered. When we have great need, or when we are praying for other people, the beams project straight from us and are immediately visible. I was also told that there is no greater prayer than that of a mother for her children. These are the purest prayers because of their intense desire and, at times, sense of desperation. A mother has the ability to give her heart to her children and to implore mightily before God for them. We all have the ability, however, to reach God with our prayers.

I understood that once our prayers of desire have been released, we need to let go of them and trust in the power of God to answer them. He knows our needs at all times and is simply waiting for an invitation to help us. He has all power to answer prayers, but he is bound by his own law and by our wills. We must invite his will to become our own. We must trust him. Once we have asked with sincere desire, doubting nothing, we will receive.

Our prayers for others have great strength but can only be answered as far as they do not infringe on the others' free will—or as long as they do not frustrate others' needs. God is bound to let us act for ourselves, but he is also willing to help in any way possible. If the faith of our friends is weak, the strength of our spirits can literally hold them up. If they are sick, our prayers of faith can often give them strength to be healed, unless their illness is appointed as a growing experience. If their death seems near, we must always remember to ask for God's will to be done, otherwise we could frustrate the person making their transition by creating in them a conflict of purpose. The range of our help for others is immense. We can do far more good for our families, friends, or others than we ever imagined.

This all seemed so simple—too simple to me at first. I had always thought prayer was an exercise of hours. I thought that we had to nag the Lord and to continue nagging him until something happened. I had my own system. I would start out by asking for something that I thought I needed. Then I would resort to bribing, hinting that it was in his best interests to help me. Then, if that failed, I would start bargaining, offering some specific act of obedience or sacrifice that would earn me his blessing. Then, in desperation, I would beg, and then, when all else failed, I would throw a tantrum. This system had generated far fewer answers to my prayers than I had hoped for. Now I understood that my prayers had been demonstrations of doubt. These ploys were the result of my lack of faith in his willingness to answer me based on the merits of my needs alone. I doubted that he was fair or even able, and I wasn't even sure if he was listening to me. All these doubts created a barrier between me and God.

Now I understood that God not only hears our prayers, but he knows our needs well before we do. I saw that he and his angels answer our prayers willingly. I saw their happiness in doing it. I saw, however, that God has a vantage point we can never perceive. He sees into our eternal pasts and futures and knows our eternal needs. In his great love he answers prayers according to this eternal and omniscient perspective. He answers *all* prayers perfectly. I saw that it was never necessary for me to repeat my requests unremittingly, as though he couldn't understand. Faith and patience are needed. He has given us our free will, and we allow his will to work in our lives when we invite him.

I also understood the importance of thanking God for the things we receive. Gratitude is an eternal virtue. In humility we must ask, and in gratitude we should receive. The more we thank God for the blessings we receive, the more we open the way for further blessings. His desire to bless us is full to overflowing. If we will open our hearts and minds to receive his blessings, we too will be filled to overflowing. We will know that he lives. We may become like the angels themselves, helping others who are in need. In prayer and service our lights will always shine. Service is the oil to our lamps generated by compassion and love.

The Council of Men

My escorts and I were still in the garden, and as I became aware again of my surroundings, my view of earth was closed. They led me from the garden to a large building. As we entered it, I was impressed with its details and exquisite beauty. Buildings are perfect there; every line and angle and detail is created to perfectly complement the entire structure, creating a feeling of wholeness or inevitability. Every structure, every creation there is a work of art.

I was led to a room, which was exquisitely built and appointed. I entered and saw a group of men seated around the long side of a kidney-shaped table. I was led to stand in front of them within the indented portion of the table. One thing struck me almost immediately; there were twelve men here—*men*—but no women.

As a rather independent thinker on earth, I was sensitive to the roles of women in the world. I was concerned about their equality and fair treatment and had very strong opinions as to their ability to compete with men on an equal footing in most settings. I might have reacted unfavorably to this council of men and no women, but I was learning to have a new perspective about the differing roles of men and women. This understanding had begun earlier while viewing the creation of the earth. I had seen then the differences between Adam and Eve. I was shown that Adam was more satisfied with his condition in the Garden and that Eve was more restless. I was shown that she wanted to become a mother desperately enough that she was willing to risk death to obtain it. Eve did not "fall" to temptation as much as she made a conscious decision to bring about conditions necessary for her progression, and her initiative was used to finally get Adam to partake of the fruit. In their partaking of the fruit, then, they brought mankind to mortality, which gave us conditions necessary for having children—but also to die.

I saw the Spirit of God resting upon Eve, and I understood that the role of women would always be unique in the world. I saw that the emotional structure of women allowed them to be more responsive to love and to allow the Spirit of God to rest upon them more fully. I understood that their roles as mothers literally gave them a special relationship to God as creators.

I also understood the peril women faced from Satan. I saw that he would use the same process of temptation in the world that had been used in the Garden. He would try to destroy families, and therefore humanity, by tempting women. This unsettled me, but I knew it was true. His plan seemed obvious. He would attack women through their restlessness, using the strength of their emotions—the same emotions that gave Eve power to move when Adam was too satisfied with his situation. I understood that he would attack the relationship between husband and wife, distancing them from each other, using the attractions of sex and greed to destroy their home. I saw that children would be damaged by broken homes and that women would then be weighed down with fear and perhaps guilt—guilt as they saw their families fall apart, and fear for the future. Satan could then use fear and guilt to destroy women and their divinely appointed purpose on earth. I was told that once Satan had the women, the men would easily follow. So, I began to see the difference in the roles between men and women, and I understood the necessity and beauty of those roles.

With this new perspective I had no reaction to the council being comprised solely of men. I accepted the fact that they had their roles and I had mine. The men radiated love for me, and I felt instantly at peace with them. They leaned together to consult with each other. Then one of them spoke to me. He said that I had died prematurely and must return to earth. I felt them saying it was *important* that I return to earth, that I had a mission to fulfill, but I resisted it in my heart. This was my home, and I felt that nothing they could say would ever convince me to leave it. The men conferred again and asked me if I wanted to review my life. The request felt almost like a command. I hesitated; no one wants their mortal past to be reviewed in this place of purity and love. They told me that it was important for me to see it, so I agreed. A light appeared to one side, and I felt the Savior's love beside me.

I stepped to my left to watch the review. It occurred in the place where I had been standing. My life appeared before me in the form of what we might consider extremely well defined holograms, but at tremendous speed. I was astonished that I could understand so much information at such a speed. My comprehension included much more than what I remember happening during each event of my life. I not only reexperienced my own emotions at each moment, but also what others around me had felt. I experienced their thoughts and feelings about me. There were times when things became clear to me in a new way. "Yes," I would say to myself. "Oh, yes. Now I see. Well, who would have guessed? But, of course, it makes sense." Then I saw the disappointment that I had caused others, and I cringed as their feelings of disappointment filled me, compounded by my own guilt. I understood all the suffering I had caused, and I felt it. I began to tremble. I saw how much grief my bad temper had caused, and I suffered this grief. I saw my selfishness, and my heart cried for relief. How had I been so uncaring?

Then in the midst of my pain, I felt the love of the council come over me. They watched my life with understanding and mercy. Everything about me was taken into consideration, how I was raised, the things I had been taught, the pain given me by others, the opportunities I had received or not received. And I realized that the council was *not judging me*. I was judging myself. Their love and mercy were absolute. Their respect for me could never be lessened. I was especially grateful for their love as the next phase of my review passed before me.

I was shown the "ripple effect," as they described it. I saw how I had often wronged people and how they had often turned to others and committed a similar wrong. This chain continued from victim to victim, like a circle of dominoes, until it came back to the start—to me, the offender. The ripples went out, and they came back. I had offended far more people than I knew, and my pain multiplied and became unbearable.

The Savior stepped toward me, full of concern and love. His spirit gave me strength, and he said that I was judging myself too critically. "You're being too harsh on yourself," he said. Then he showed me the reverse side of the ripple effect. I saw myself perform an act of kindness, just a simple act of unselfishness, and I saw the ripples go out again. The friend I had been kind to was kind in turn to one of her friends, and the chain repeated itself. I saw love and happiness increase in others' lives because of that one simple act on my part. I saw their happiness grow and affect their lives in positive ways, some significantly. My pain was replaced with joy. I *felt* the love they felt, and I felt their joy. And this from one simple act of kindness. A powerful thought hit me, and I repeated it over and over in my mind: "Love is really the only thing that matters. Love is really the only thing that matters, and love is *joy!*" I recalled the scripture that said, "I am come that they might have life, and that they might have it more abundantly" (John 10:10), and my soul was filled with this abundant joy.

It all seemed so simple. *If we're kind, we'll have joy.* And the question suddenly came out of me: "Why didn't I know this before?" Jesus or one of the men responded, and the answer was ingrained in me. It sank into the deepest part of my soul, changing my outlook on trials and opposition forever: "You needed the negative as well as the positive experiences on earth. Before you can feel joy, you must know sorrow."

All of my experiences now took on new meaning. I realized that no real mistakes had been made in my life. Each experience was a tool for me to grow by. Every unhappy experience had allowed me to obtain greater understanding about myself, until I learned to avoid those experiences. I also saw myself growing in ability to help others. I even saw that many of my experiences had been orchestrated by guardian angels. Some experiences were sad and some were joyful, but all were calculated to bring me to higher levels of knowledge. I saw that the guardian angels remained with me through my trials, helping me in any way they could. Sometimes I had many guardian angels around me, sometimes just a few, depending on my needs. In reviewing my life I saw that I often repeated the same mistakes, committing the same harmful actions over and over, until finally I learned the lesson. But I also saw that the more I learned, the more doors of opportunity were opened to me. And they were literally *opened*. Many things I thought I had done by myself were shown to have been extended by divine help.

So the review quickly changed from a negative experience to a very positive one. My perspective of myself was changed, and I saw my sins and shortcomings in a multi-dimensional light. Yes, they were grievous to me and others, but they were tools for me to learn by, to correct my thinking and behavior. I understood that forgiven sins are blotted out. It is as if they are overlaid by new understanding, by a new direction in life. This new understanding then leads me to naturally abandon the sin. Although the sin is blotted out, however, the educational part of the experience remains. Thus the forgiven sin helps me to grow and increases my ability to help others.

This expanded knowledge gave me the perspective I needed to truly forgive myself. And I understood that forgiveness of self is where all forgiveness starts. If I am unable to forgive myself, it is impossible for me to truly forgive others. And I *must* forgive others. What I give out is what I receive. If I want forgiveness, I have to give forgiveness. I also saw that the behavior in others that I criticized most—and forgave least—was almost always a behavior that I myself possessed, or feared having. I was threatened by others' examples of my own weaknesses, or by my potential weaknesses.

I saw how damaging lust for the things of this world can be. All real growth occurs spiritually, and worldly things like possessions and rampant appetites smother the spirit. They become our gods, binding us to the flesh, and we are not free to experience the growth and joy that God desires for us.

I was told again, not in words this time but by understanding, that the most important thing I could do in life was to love others as myself. But to love others as myself, I first had to really love myself. The beauty and light of Christ were within me—he saw it!—and now I had to search within myself to find it as well. As if this were a commandment, I did just this, and I saw that I had suppressed the genuine loveliness of my own soul. I had to let it shine again as it once had.

My review was over, and the men sat in stillness, radiating their absolute love for me. The Savior was there in his light, smiling, pleased with my progress. The men then conferred again and turned back to me. "You have not completed your mission on earth," they said. "You must go back. But, we will not compel you; the choice is yours."

Without hesitation, I said, "No, no. I can't go back. I belong here. This is my home." I stood firm, knowing that nothing could ever make me choose to leave.

One of the men spoke, also firmly. "Your work is not complete. It is best that you return."

I was *not* going back. I had learned as a child how to win a fight, and now I employed all those skills. I threw myself down and began crying. "I *won't* go back," I wailed, "and nobody is going to make me! I'm staying right here where I belong. I'm *through* with earth!"

Jesus stood not far from me, off to my right, still glowing in his brilliant light. He came forward now, and I felt his concern. But mixed with his concern was a sense of amusement. He still delighted in me, understanding my moods, and I sensed his empathy for my desire to stay. I arose, and he said to the council, "Let us show her what her mission involves." Then turning back to me he said: "Your mission will be made known to you so that you might make a clearer decision. But after this, you must decide. If you return to your life on earth, your mission and much of what you have been shown will be removed from your memory."

Reluctantly I agreed and was shown my mission.

Afterward, I knew that I had to come back. Although I would hate to leave that glorious world of light and love for one of hardship and uncertainty, the necessity of my mission compelled me to return. But first, I received a promise from each person present, including Jesus. I made them promise that the moment my mission was complete they would take me back home. I was not willing to spend a minute on earth longer than was necessary. My home was with them. They agreed to my terms, and things were put in motion for my return.

The Savior then came to me and told me of his pleasure in my decision. He reminded me that when I returned to earth I would not remember what I had seen concerning my mission. "While on the earth you are not to dwell on what your mission is," he said. "It will be done according to its time."

"Oh, he knows me so well!" I thought. I knew that if I did remember my mission while on earth, I would complete it as rapidly, and probably as ineffectively, as possible. It was done according to the Savior's words. The details of my mission have been removed from my memory. Not even a hint remains, and strangely, I have no desire to dwell on it.

As for the Lord's promise to take me the moment my mission is complete, his last words to me still ring in my ears: "The days of the earth are short. You will not be long there, and you will return here."

The Farewell

*S*uddenly thousands of angels surrounded me. They were exuberant, pleased that I had made the decision to return. I heard their cheering, supporting me with love and encouragement.

As I looked about, my heart melting for the love I felt from them, they began to sing. No music I had heard in my life, even the music in the garden, compared to this. It was grand, glorious, awesome, and meant especially for me. It was overwhelming. They sang spontaneously, parts not so much memorized as instantly known, instantly felt. Their voices were pure and each note was clear and sweet. I do not remember the song they sang, but I was told that I would hear them sing again. I wept openly, soaking in their love and celestial music—hardly believing that an insignificant soul like my own could be at the center of so much adoration. And I knew that no one is insignificant in the eternities. Every soul is of infinite worth. As my spirit swelled with humility and gratitude, I saw one last vision of the earth.

When the heavens scrolled back, I saw the earth with its billions of people on it. I saw them scrambling for existence, making mistakes, experiencing kindness, finding love, grieving for death, and I saw the angels hovering above them. The angels knew the people by name and watched over them closely. They cheered when good was done and were saddened by mistakes. They hovered about to help and give direction and protection. I saw that we could literally call down thousands of angels in our aid if we ask in faith. I saw that we are *all* equal in their eyes, great or small, talented or handicapped, leaders or followers, saints or sinners. We are all precious and carefully watched over. Their love never fails us.

The vision closed and I gazed one last time at my eternal friends, the two women who had guided me, my three faithful ministering angels, and many others whom I had known and loved. They were magnificent, noble, and glorious, and I knew that I had only seen a glimpse of their souls. I had been privileged to view only a tiny vestibule of heaven, just a part of that paradisiacal home. Knowledge beyond my deepest dreams existed there and in the hearts of those who dwell there. Plans, paths, and truths await us there, some of which are eternities old, and some of which we have yet to make. I have been shown a glimpse of the things of heaven, and I will always treasure that glimpse. I knew that the angels singing now, filling my heart with love, would be my last glorious experience in this world. And as they continued to express their love and support for me, I began to cry. I was going home.

My Return

No good-byes were said; I simply found myself in the hospital room again. The door was still half open, the light was on above the sink, and lying on the bed under the blankets was my body. I stood in the air and looked down at it and was filled with revulsion. It looked cold and heavy and reminded me of an old pair of coveralls that had been dragged through mud and grime. In comparison, I felt like I had just taken a long, soothing shower, and now I had to put that heavy, cold, muddy garment on. But I knew I had to do it—I had promised—but I had to hurry. If I thought about it one second longer I would lose courage and flee. Quickly, my spirit slipped back into the body. Once made, the commitment to go through with it was a natural process over which I had little control.

The body's cumbersome weight and coldness were abhorrent. I started jerking around inside it as though many volts of electricity were pulsing through me. I felt the pain and sickness of my body again, and I became inconsolably depressed. After the joy of spiritual freedom, I had become a prisoner to the flesh again.

As I lay trapped in the body, my three ancient friends appeared by my bed again. My dear monks, my ministering spirits, had come to comfort me. I was so terribly weak that I could not greet them as I wanted to. They were my last hold on the loveliness and purity of where I had been, and I wanted with all my heart to reach out to them and thank them for their sweet and eternal friendship. I wanted to say one more time: "I love you." But I could only stare through eyes filling with tears and hope they understood.

There was no need to speak; they understood all. And silently they stood near me, looking into my eyes, radiating their love, filling me with a spirit that conquered all pain. For a few precious seconds we looked into each other's eyes and communicated heart to heart. In those moments they gave me a message that I will always treasure as a sacred token of our everlasting friendship. Their words and presence gave me great comfort. I knew that they knew not only my feelings but the path of my new life, the pain I would endure for the loss of their love, the frustrations of earth life again, the difficult journeys ahead. They were pleased with my decision to come back to earth. I had made the right choice. "But for now," they said, "rest awhile." And they produced a very peaceful and quieting feeling. I felt it flow over me, and I began immediately to fall into a deep and healing sleep. As I drifted off, I felt beauty and love envelop me.

I don't know how long I slept. When I opened my eyes again it was two a.m. It had been over four hours since my death. How much of that time I had spent in the spirit world I did not know, but four hours didn't seem nearly long enough for all that had happened to me. I didn't know if any medical action had been taken to revive me, or even if anyone had been in to see me. I felt rested now, but still I could not shake off my deep depression. Then I began to relive my experience, letting it all pass through my mind, and I was filled with wonder that I had actually visited with the Savior of the world and been held in his arms. I began to feel stronger as I reflected on the knowledge I had received while in his presence, and I knew his light would continue to give me strength and comfort in hours of need.

I was about to close my eyes and drift off to sleep when I caught a movement by the door. I tried to raise up on an elbow to get a better look, and I saw a creature poke its head in. I cringed backward in fear. Then another one appeared. They were creatures of the most hideous and grotesque appearance imaginable. Five of them entered the doorway, and I was all but paralyzed with fear. They appeared to be half-human half-animal—short, muscular beings with long claws or fingernails and savage, though human, faces. They came toward me, snarling, growling, and hissing. They were full of hate, and I knew that they intended to kill me. I tried to scream but was either too weak or too paralyzed with fear to move. I was helpless as they came to within five or six feet of the bed.

Suddenly a huge dome of light, almost like glass, fell over me, and the creatures lunged forward, seeming to recognize its threat to them. The dome protected me as they frantically flailed at it and tried to climb on it to get a better vantage point. But the dome was too high to climb on, and they became more frustrated. They shrieked and cursed and hissed and began spitting. I was horrified as I felt trapped in my bed. The creatures were persistent, and I didn't know if the dome could hold up. I didn't even know what it was.

When I thought I could bear it no more and my fear seemed about to overwhelm me, my three adoring angels, the monks, entered the room again, and the creatures fled. The angels said not to fear, that I was protected. They told me that the devil was angry at my decision to return to earth and that he had sent these powerful demons to destroy me. They explained that the dome would remain around me for the rest of my life. They said that the demons might try to get at me again and that I might see or hear them in the future, but the dome would protect me. "Also know," they said, "that we are always near you to help and encourage you." Moments later, to my sadness, the monks were gone.

This was my last visit with my three ministering angels. I lovingly call them my monks, but I know that they are three of my closest friends in all eternity. I look forward with anxious heart to the day we can embrace each other again and renew our eternal friendship.

The demons came again after the angels left, but the dome kept them from me. I reached for the phone and called my husband and began to explain that there were demons in my room. He thought I was hallucinating and got one of our daughters to talk to me on the phone while he hurriedly drove to the hospital. Ten minutes later Joe walked through the doorway. He could not see the creatures in the room, but he came to the side of my bed and held my hand while I tried to tell him what was happening. Soon the creatures became frustrated and left again, not to return that night. I was relieved and began to calm down. Then I tried to tell Joe a little about my death experience. I didn't go into much detail then, but he knew that something significant had happened, and he was full of love and concern for me. The angels may have departed, but Joe was now there, comforting and protecting me. The love I felt from him may not have been as powerful as that from the angels or from Christ, but it was marvelous and very comforting nonetheless. The love we share as mortals may be imperfect, but it still has great power to heal and sustain.

My Return

As Joe stayed with me, my spirit traveled in and out of both worlds, as if my return had not been made permanent. I remember doctors and nurses working on me; I didn't know what they were doing, or even how long they had been there, but I sensed the tension and anxiety in their efforts. I continued to view the spirit world during this time, and I saw many wonderful things—things of both this world and the other. Then I received another powerful experience, not in the form of a vision, but a visitation.

A beautiful little girl came into the room. She was only two or three years old and was the only child that I had seen in the spirit. A golden halo of light emanated from her, glowing in the room wherever she walked. She seemed quite attracted to Joe, and while the doctors and nurses were out of the room for a moment I asked him if he could see her. He couldn't. She had the grace of a ballerina, walking almost on the tips of her toes and performing little gestures, as though she were dancing. I was struck immediately by her spontaneity and happiness. She went to Joe and stood on the toe of his shoe. She balanced on one foot and kicked her other leg up behind her like a ballerina might, and leaned forward to reach into his pants pocket. I was mesmerized by this movement. I asked her what she was doing. She turned and laughed, smiling in an impish way, and I knew that she had heard me. But she didn't reply. I sensed her inner joy, the pure, exuberant happiness that filled her inside. She then faded from my view and never reappeared, but I knew I would never forget her.

For the next few hours nurses and doctors were in and out, checking on me. Although they were paying much more attention to me than they had the night before, neither Joe nor I shared anything of my experience with them. The next morning one of the doctors said, "You really had a hard time last night. Can you tell me what you experienced?" I found that I couldn't share it with him, and I said I had nightmares. I was discovering that it was difficult for me to talk about my journey beyond, and it wasn't long before I didn't even want to share more of it with Joe. Talking seemed to dilute it. The experience was sacred. A few weeks passed and I did share more of it with Joe and the older children. They immediately supported me, dispelling any fears I had of telling my family what had happened. I had a lot of learning and growing to do in the years ahead. In fact, the next few years would be the most difficult of my life.

My Recovery

I began sinking into a deep depression. I couldn't forget the scenes of beauty and peace of the spirit world, and I wanted terribly to return there. As the world whirled around me, I became fearful of life, even loathing it at times, praying for death. I asked God to take me home, to please, please release me from this life and unknown mission. I became agoraphobic, fearing to leave the house. I remember times when I would look out the window to the mailbox and wish that I had the courage to go to it. I was sinking into myself, dying a slow death, and although Joe and the children were wonderfully supportive, I knew that I was slipping away from them.

Finally it was love for my family that saved me. I realized my self-pity was not fair to them. I *had* to join life again, make myself leave the spirit world behind and move on. I forced myself out of the house and gradually became involved in my children's activities—school work, charitable service, church groups, camping, family vacations, and so on. It didn't happen all at once, but life became enjoyable again. Although my heart never truly left the spirit world, my love for this life flourished and became stronger than ever.

Five years after my death experience I felt a desire to go back to the hospital to find out what might have happened to me physically that night. Until then the doctors had never said, and I had never asked. I had shared my experience with a few friends by then, and they all seemed to ask the same thing: "But did the *doctors* know you were dead?" I didn't need the doctors' confirmation to know that I had died—Jesus himself told me I had—but my friends wanted more information. I made an appointment to see the doctor who performed the operation, and I went to his office. The lobby was crowded with ladies waiting to see him; his nurse said that he was running late. I felt ashamed for taking his valuable time—these other people needed him more than I did. I waited anyway and was eventually led to his office.

When he came in, he remembered me and asked how he could help. I reminded him of the operation, and he said he remembered it. Then I said that I needed to know the truth about any complications that might have arisen the night after the surgery. He asked me why I needed to know, and I began to relate portions of the experience. Forty-five minutes passed. The lobby was jammed with people still waiting for him, but the doctor didn't move. I concluded, explaining that I wasn't interested in seeking a lawsuit; I just wanted to know what went wrong—that it meant a lot to me to know. Without speaking, he stood and went to his files. When he came back, tears filled his eyes. Yes, he said, there were complications that night; they *had* lost me for a while but had felt that it was best not to mention anything to me. Then he went on to explain what had happened. I had hemorrhaged during the operation, and it appeared that the hemorrhage occurred again later that night. At the time of my death, I had been left alone during the nurses' shift change, and because I was unattended, they didn't know exactly how long I had been dead. The doctor and nurses worked on me, giving me an injection, more medication, and I.V.s through the rest of the morning. After listening to the doctor, I was satisfied that he and the attending staff had done all they could for me.

I asked the doctor why he was crying, and he said that his tears were tears of happiness. He had recently lost a loved one and found hope in my story. My experience of a world beyond this one gave him solace. He also said that he remembered a similar experience from another patient some years before, and many of the details were the same. He was comforted in knowing that life did not end with death and that we will meet our family members again. I assured him that there was great reason to hope for a glorious life beyond this one—a life far more glorious than we imagine.

When I left his office, I felt free. I could leave the details of my physical death behind me forever. And to others I could truthfully say what I had always known: I had in fact died, and had returned.

My Special Angel

A year after visiting with the doctor, six years after my experience, my sister Dorothy called with an unusual story. She told me about a woman who was expecting a baby that would be put up for adoption. The woman and her husband were alcoholics and one child had already been removed from them for previous problems. Unfortunately, the family that had taken the first child had too many children and could not accept this one. Because the baby was a Native American, they wanted to keep it in a family of Native American parents, preferably within its own extended family.

Dorothy knew that I had been depressed for some time and thought that keeping my hands busy with another baby—this would be my eighth—would help me get back to normal. She said they needed someone to take the baby for a couple of months. I discussed it with Joe and the family, and although I had just registered at the community college to begin work on a college degree, I found myself considering it. My daughter, Cheryl, was expecting a baby and said that she would come over every day to help me so that she could get used to taking care of an infant. Joe said that he wouldn't mind holding a little one again—our youngest was twelve. I said yes, and by the time the case worker brought the darling baby girl to our home, I had everything ready for it; we had found the old cradle that we were saving for our grandchildren and other odds and ends that our own babies had used. I instantly took to her, creating a bond that I knew would be difficult to break. I kept reminding myself that she would be leaving soon, but what my head kept saying, my heart denied.

The court was having trouble finding an adoptive home within the child's immediate family. Two months passed. My daughter had a baby boy, and I visited them as often as possible, taking my foster daughter with me.

She was cheerful, bright, and always wanted hugs. When she felt ill or wanted comfort, she dug her nose into my neck and let my breath fall on her face. This often quieted her when nothing else would. Of course, the whole family loved her. In the mornings, our twelve- and fourteen-year-old boys would steal her out of her crib and take her into the family room to play games with her.

She began to walk at ten months, and her olive complexion was as healthy and glowing as any baby's. I smoothed her down every morning with lotion until her skin was soft as silk, and throughout the day I loved to smell it on her. My love for her deepened over the months, and soon I forgot that she wasn't mine.

She was ten and a half months old when the case worker called to tell me that they had found relatives for her in another state. The adoptive parents would be by in a few days to pick her up. I was stunned. Joe and I had signed an agreement saying that we would not attempt adoption, and now I was desperate. We had known all along she couldn't be ours, but now I was in the worst agony a mother can know. I was about to lose my child.

I packed her clothing in a misty cloud of numbness. People spoke to me, but I did not hear them. Questions raced through my mind seeking answers not to be found. I had never believed that I would become so emotionally attached—so much in love. How had I let it happen? Where was my strength to let go?

When the new parents drove up, I carried her to the car. At first she thought that *we* were going somewhere, and she happily nuzzled me and said "bye-bye" to the rest of our family. They were in the same stupor that enveloped me. The adoptive parents waited in the car and didn't say anything. I was grateful for that. No one could have said anything to give me comfort then. When the new mother reached for my baby, my heart slid up and tightened around my throat. I wanted to run with the baby, run and never stop; but my legs wouldn't move. They were weak and shaking.

The baby realized that she was being taken away from me and began to scream. My heart broke. As the car drove off, I stood immobile. The vision of my precious little girl crying with hands outstretched, reaching for me, burned into my soul. I broke down and ran into the house, the image searing me. It was to torment me for months to come.

Everything in the house reminded me of her—the piano where she loved to sit and pretend that she was mommy, the playpen filled with toys, the crib with her empty bottle in it. And most of all, the stillness.

After three months I could bear it no more, and I began praying to the Lord to return her to me. The memories were too deep, too fresh, too inconsolable. Nobody spoke of her, but I knew the entire family was in pain; we all needed her. Then one night after my spirit had been broken down by the realization that she wasn't returning, I prayed for the family that had her. I asked our Father in Heaven to bless them so that they could make her happy. I asked him to bless her that she could accept her new surroundings and find peace of mind and joy. I prayed with all my heart for that family and their precious little daughter. Then, feeling at last that it was in the Lord's hands, I finally drifted off to sleep.

That night I was awakened by a messenger who stood by my bed. I understood that he had come from the spirit world. He said that the situation with my baby was not right, that she would be returned to me. He said that I would receive a phone call in which the caller would say, "I have good news, and I have bad news." I did not sleep the rest of the night.

For the next two weeks I would not leave the house. Every time the phone rang I jumped for it, waiting for that special call. I told Dorothy about the messenger, but I couldn't bring myself to tell the rest of the family, not even Joe. I felt like I had already tried their patience enough. Even Dorothy was wondering about me.

The phone rang early one morning, and I heard a voice plainly say, "Betty, this is Ellen. I have some good news, and I have some bad news." I sat up in bed and screamed, "Wait! Wait a minute!" I had been asleep and thought I was dreaming. I crawled out of bed and looked in the mirror to make sure I was awake, then I grabbed the phone and said, "Okay, I'm listening." My heart was pounding so hard that it pulsed against my eardrums. The voice continued, explaining that my baby was in a hospital. "She wouldn't adjust to the new family," Ellen said, "and she kept crying. You were her mommy for ten months, and she's been looking for you."

Ellen went on to explain that as the baby cried, tempers rose, and one night in a drunken rage the parents beat her and threw her down a flight of stairs. The baby had then been taken to a hospital and abandoned, where she lay critically ill for two weeks. She was not responding to treatment and the doctors recognized that in her emotional state she might never recover. Finally Ellen said, "Betty, our last hope is you. We know we're asking a lot, but could you please take her back for a while, at least until she gets better?"

I felt faint, and my breath came in gasps. "Can I call you right back?" I asked. Then I hung up the phone. It was seven-thirty, and Joe had already gone to work. I ran to the stairs and screamed for the kids. I told them I had wonderful news, but then I couldn't get it out. My throat tightened, the words would not pass through my lips. The children followed me to the phone and listened as I called Joe and tried to tell him what had happened. He said he'd be home right away. His voice was calmer than mine and that comforted me. I was starting to feel revived a little, and I realized that I hadn't given Ellen an answer—in my excitement I had practically hung up on her. I re-dialed her number, then I became panicky that I had misunderstood her. What if everything had been a mistake? She answered, and I asked her to repeat everything again, which she did, adding that she was flying to the city where the baby had been abandoned. I told her that I would go with her, but she said it wouldn't be appropriate—to wait here. But she had told me where the baby was, and right after she hung up I dialed the travel agency and made plans to be on the same flight with her. I called her back and said I was going with her. Reluctantly, she said that she would meet me at the airport. Another case worker would meet us in the other city, bringing the baby with him. The flight was too long, and as soon we were let off the plane I ran into the terminal and began searching through crowds for my baby.

Knowing the case worker was a man, I looked for a single male with a child. I couldn't find them, and I began feeling frantic. I knew exactly what the baby looked like; why couldn't I find her? Then to one side I spotted them, but the baby in his arms didn't resemble the image in my memories at all. Still, I *knew* it was her. "That's my baby!" I heard myself screaming as I ran to them and snatched her out of his arms.

The baby was bald except for tufts of hair here and there. Her eyes were swollen, and one eyebrow was cut and bruised. She recognized me immediately and clutched me tightly, with both her arms and little legs wrapped tightly around me. "What have they done? What have they done?" I cried. The case worker was surprised at this strange, crying woman who had pulled the baby from his arms. Ellen came up behind me and explained to him that it was all right, that I was the baby's mother.

Joe and all six children met us at the airport on our return. Their eyes lit up in excitement and filled with tears when they saw the little bundle in my arms. The baby saw them and willingly went to each of them as they reached to hold her. But she stayed with each only briefly, needing to return to me between hugs. She clung to me like her life depended on my existence.

For the next few months she wouldn't let me leave her sight. We became aware of the harm that had been done to her fragile emotions. She wouldn't speak to anybody, she refused to walk, and her face was expressionless. The only time she made a sound was when I left her. Then she cried until I returned. Finally, I wrapped her in a dish towel and tied her to my body so I could get some work done around the house. She and I spent a few months tied together like this. I put her crib next to my bed and retired early each night, because she refused to go to sleep without me next to her. At first her crib was right next to my bed, and I put my hand through the bars and held her hand until she fell asleep. As the months went by, I moved her crib a little farther away each night until she was eventually able to sleep on the other side of the room.

Joe and I had hired an attorney to begin immediate adoption proceedings. We had also taken her to a hospital for an examination to document the abuse she had experienced. We found that besides the obvious cuts and bruises, she had suffered a fractured arm, dehydration, malnourishment, and had sores on her scalp where clumps of her hair had been torn out. Her mental condition could only be guessed at, but her desperate clinging to me and refusal of others showed deep distrust. The doctor saw that her health depended on the continuous, stable family life she received with us.

The court reviewed the matter and considered all the evidence. The decision was soon in coming: she was ours. Joe wanted to change her name, wanting to give her the most precious name he knew, and even though I objected, the family overruled me. They couldn't miss the similarities in personality and the deep bonding that we had established; she was legally renamed Betty Jean, after me, her new mother.

By the time little Betty was two and a half, she had fully recovered both physically and emotionally. She became once again the most darling and playful child in the house, surprising us constantly with her quick sense of humor. One afternoon she ran over to Joe. As an impish smile came to her face, she stood up on the toe of his shoe, threw her other foot up behind her, and balancing like a ballerina reached up to dig into the pocket of his slacks. A chill ran through me as memories flooded back. Little Betty laughed, and I heard the voice of a little girl years before, a little girl who had kept us company in a hospital room when heaven and earth seemed one. Then I saw and understood more. A vision of a young woman came back to me, a memory of a beautiful and energetic spirit who had once been waiting to come to earth. I remembered her as the young spirit with whom I shared a bond in a previous time, the one in the spirit world whose loveliness and energy captivated me. I wanted to cry as every-

thing about this precious angel came together. I had
been allowed to see her as a child in the spirit. Now
I knew why I had been shown her as an adult spirit
ready to come to earth. I knew also that while she
could not be born to me because of my hysterectomy,
she had found another way to become a part of my
life. And now I knew why I had been compelled to
take her as a baby. We were closest of friends forever,
eternities of experiences behind us, and eternities
ahead.

My family has grown since these experiences, and
most of them have left home. They have begun their
own families and embarked on their own paths of
progression. Joe and I still try to help them through
painful moments, but we know that we can never live
their lives for them and would not want to. We
understand that they are heavenly beings like ourselves, here for an earthly experience. We can't
swallow up their sorrow, and we can't plan their joy.
All we can do is be family. All we can do is *love*.

More experiences have come to me since November 18, 1973, but I am reluctant to share them here;
it took nineteen years and countless proddings to get

me to share the experiences in this book. Everything has its time; for this book, the time is now.

I've wondered from time to time just what my mission would entail, but of course, no understanding has come, no answers offered. I have simply been impressed to live within the light of Jesus Christ and to continue to accept his love in my life. By doing this, I suppose, I will be able to do all that he may want of me.

We are to love one another. I know that. We are to be kind, to be tolerant, to give generous service. I know that greater joy will come to us through love than in any other way. I have seen its wonderful, glorious rewards. The details of my experience are important only to the point that they help us to love. All else is an appendage to that. It is simply a matter of following the Savior's message which he most clearly expressed to me: "Above all else, love one another."

I will continue to try.

and Holly Beth read this
book 1/28/94 !